FLYING FOX

FLYINGFOX

A BUSINESS ADVENTURE IN TEAMS AND TEAMWORK

JOHN BUTMAN

American Management Association

New York • Atlanta • Boston • Chicago • Kansas City • San Francisco • Washington, D.C.
Brussels • Toronto • Mexico City

Library of Congress Cataloging-in-Publication Data

Butman, John.
    FlyingFox : a business adventure in teams and teamwork / John
Butman.
        p.   cm.
    ISBN 0–8144–5099–7
    1. Work groups.   I. Title.
HD66.B87   1993
658.4'02—dc20   92-40254
                                                                       CIP

Printing number

10   9   8   7   6   5   4   3   2   1

Contents

Acknowledgments

Thanks to the dozens of people who have shared their corporate tales, ideas, and experiences with me over the years.

Thanks to my advisers and early readers, including Biff Burns, Frank Dramis, Shirlee Finley, Jim Hannum, Dan Johnson, Paul Kent, George Lynde, Kate Miller, Jack Nevison, Mike Potter, Rob Stein, and Tom Wilson.

Thanks to John Guaspari for introducing me to AMACOM Books.

Thanks to Myles Thompson, my editor, who is peerless in so many ways.

And thanks to my scrappy and unpredictable—but winning—family team, Nancy, Jeremy, and Henry.

The Company

Fungible Company Incorporated (FCI) was founded in 1951 by Dr. Marshall Osgood. It is organized into six operating groups and conducts business in a variety of market segments in some fifty-three countries worldwide.

The Characters

(in nonhierarchical alphabetical order by first name)

At FCI

Asvinkumar Prandar—software developer
Bill Ferry—CEO
Dick Eggart—Ficus team leader
Emil Zanoski (Dr. Z)—chief of R&D
Jasper Lash—technology systems group chief
Jocelyn Veens—MIS director
Martha Morgan—C&P group chief
Marshall Osgood—founder and board member emeritus

FlyingFox Team

Andrea Carnovale—marketing specialist
Carlos Garcia—manufacturing director
Cub Wilson—sales
Kate Fiersen—marketing communications director
Nelson Favreau—manufacturing manager
Nick Yu—R&D engineer
Phyllis Burch—purchaser
Ron Delaney—FlyingFox team leader
Wesley Dunn—engineering manager

At Shark Design

Hartmut Horst—owner and creative director
Keith Levy—design engineer

Ron's Family

Emma Delaney—Ron's daughter
Janice Delaney—Ron's wife
Kip Delaney—Ron's son

Part I

1. *Welcome to the New World.*

At two o'clock on a Thursday afternoon in April, our recently anointed president and CEO, Bill Ferry, was scheduled to speak to us in the cafeteria of the Old Building. I left my office on the fifth floor of Building Three a few minutes before two, intending to grab a frozen yogurt before Ferry got started.

Everyone else had the same idea, however, and so I joined a long line of FCI managers, plastic trays in hand, at the food counter. Dick Eggart, just ahead of me, sensed my six-foot-two inches of managerial presence looming above his five-foot-ten inches of financial expertise.

Dick turned and brightened. "Hey, Ron!"

"Hi, Dick. Count a lot of beans today?" I used that distinctive corporate conversational tone that is equal parts honey and venom and that can take years of practice to perfect.

"Yeah, but I'm still waiting for a few numbers from you, Ron."

"I know," I said, wishing I had not asked the question—I was a day late in delivering my next-quarter forecasts. "I'll get them to you tomorrow." I pointed ahead. The line was advancing and Dick was not.

"Just try to make them realistic." Dick slid forward a couple of steps. "Ferry is not into numbers games."

"I always do."

"You know what I mean." Dick changed the subject. "What's this all about, do you know?" He waved his hand in the direction of the temporary platform at the far end of the cafeteria, where people were bustling around a podium and microphone.

"If *you* don't know, we're in trouble," I said. Dick is a genuine Fickie, as only the most loyal and longest-serving FCI employee is called. He was a lifer, a fixture in finance and extremely well connected. I was a mere six-year veteran. If Dick didn't have inside information on this meeting, something had gone awry with the traditional channels of communication.

Dick leaned toward me conspiratorially. "I think Ferry's planning a reorganization. That's what he did when he took over FCI Europe."

"Well, we could use a little shaking up."

Dick shivered. "Not if it means going through another purge." The Purge was Fickie jargon for the program of belt tightening, consolidating, and semiforced early retirements that Ferry's predecessor had instituted about two years ago.

"It wasn't so bad," I said, nodding Dick forward once again. "You've got to clean house now and again."

"It was bad if you lost friends in it. Or discretionary funds."

We had reached the yogurt dispenser at last and Dick studied the available flavors. There was a click from the microphone.

"Ladies and gentlemen! Good afternoon! Could you please take your seats. It's two o'clock and we're ready to get started." The equable, medium-pitched voice was unfamiliar. Dick and I—the entire line, in fact—turned and saw that the voice belonged to Bill Ferry himself.

Dick hesitated for a second, his fingers poised longingly on the lever of the flavor of the day, cherry chocolate swirl. We looked at each other and shrugged. This was no time for yogurt. We joined the exodus from the food line to the folding chairs, parting company in the rush. I slipped into one of the few remaining aisle seats and immediately felt a hand on my shoulder.

"Move your skinny ass over, Ronnie." The hand belonged to Kate Fiersen, director of marketing communications. A great swoop of blond hair. Perpetual tan. Impeccable knit outfit, accessorized with jewelry to the limit of corporate acceptability. Kate, the Pistol, Queen of marcomms. Out of sheer orneriness, I considered making her squeeze past my knees, which were squashed uncomfortably into the back of the seat in front of me. I decided against it, however; Kate was capable of converting even the most minor of slights into a murderous feud that could rage on for years.

"My great pleasure, Kate," I said and slid over.

"Thanks, Ron." She alit, crossed her legs, and began flicking the well-manicured nail of her right index finger against her left thumbnail. It made a sharp, imperious, impatient noise.

"Ferry better get a stronger start here than he did in Europe," Kate said under her breath. She had worked overseas

4

for years, first in Australia and then at FCI Europe, based in Paris. She was there when Ferry was promoted from executive vice-president to president.

I agreed. "He's taken his time to talk to us. It's been four months since he got here."

"He wanted to make damned sure he had a solid program," she said. "And damned sure he had his senior people on board. That's what happened to him in Europe. He went public with a reorganization, and some of his top guys didn't support him."

"I thought he was the wonder boy over there."

"He was. But he wasted a lot of time begging and appeasing people he should have dumped at the beginning. Besides, he had a boom market. It's different now. No way is the board going to give him the luxury of time over here. He's got to move fast. And he's got to start by making a good impression on the top girls and boys of TSG." Today's audience—about 150 managers—came from the Technology Systems Group (TSG), the oldest, largest, and most influential group at FCI, the spiritual center of the company.

I caught sight of Dick Eggart a few rows ahead of me. "A lot of people won't be impressed if he starts by announcing a reorganization."

Kate glanced at me, knowingly. "But *you* wouldn't mind, would you, Ronnie? Maverick that you are."

"I'd keep an open mind."

Kate patted me condescendingly on the wrist. "Ron, I really doubt that anybody who's tall, cute, *and* has red hair can possess an open mind as well."

I was about to protest that my hair is more strawberry-brown than red, when Ferry stepped up to the mike. "Ladies and gentlemen! Good afternoon!"

All eyes forward. Ferry is a tall, lean man with a combination of athleticism and intelligence that reminds me of a tennis ace (which he is, as well as an instrument-rated pilot and a decent oboe player). Although he is in his late forties, his sandy hair and boyish voice make him seem more like thirty-five. He removed the mike from its stand and stepped out from behind the podium.

"Thank you all for coming this afternoon. I'm honored to

be here in one of the world's finest cafeterias, home of the celebrated Fickie Roll." Murmur of laughter from the audience. The Old Building cafeteria does its baking in-house, and the bakery's plump, sugary coffee rolls have become famous throughout FCI.

Kate leaned to me and whispered, "Nice. The common touch. Shows he's got good local knowledge."

"Mm." I was not particularly interested in listening to Kate's running commentary on Ferry's speech.

Ferry continued. "Some of you may not realize that although I've been CEO of FCI U.S. for just four months, I've been with the company for almost eighteen years now. I started out on the West Coast in engineering. I did a stint in sales in the southeastern region. Then I spent several years in the Europe, Africa, and Middle East operation in a variety of positions, and I ended up as president of FCI Europe for three years before I came back to the fold."

Ferry paused and looked out over the audience. He was completely natural on stage, and spoke as if he had all the time in the world.

"I know I've kept a low profile the last few months and some of you have been wondering what I've been doing all that time. Well, I've been busy getting to know what's going on. I've visited most of our facilities in North America. I've talked with FCI people in every discipline. I've learned a great deal about our products and programs. I've met with dozens of customers. I've done a lot of listening. And I must say that I have been tremendously impressed by what I have seen and the people I've met."

He paused again and took a few steps across the stage.

"Here comes the *but*," Kate whispered.

"However, I don't think it's any secret that we're not as successful now as we have been in the past or as we'd like to be in the future. To be sure, we're competing in an extremely competitive global marketplace. But that's a given. And it doesn't explain or excuse the reality of our situation today. What is the reality? In key markets, we're slowly losing share. On key products, our profitability is eroding. At TSG, in particular, we are threatened in our bread-and-butter market, office systems. Most important, we're not creating enough *new* products. And

6

the ones we are developing often get to market late. Do these factors mean we're in a critical position?"

Pause. The room was silent.

"Everybody's peeing in their pants now," whispered Kate.

"Yes, they do," continued Ferry. "We're not in serious trouble yet. We are still the leader in some markets. We have a healthy balance sheet and tremendously valuable assets. Overall, we're profitable. But if we don't move quickly, we *will* be in trouble. TSG's position in the office systems market is already in trouble. And in the long run, FCI's survival could even be threatened."

There was an uncomfortable shifting of bodies throughout the audience. Ferry waited for everyone to settle.

"What has caused this erosion of our success? I said a moment ago that I've met a lot of talented and effective people in the past few months. And I believe that. This is not a matter of placing blame or finding scapegoats."

"Tell that to the two VPs he canned," Kate whispered in my ear. Two senior vice-presidents had left the company soon after Ferry had arrived, but they had slipped away quietly and weeks apart. There had been a little speculation at the time that it was Ferry who had forced them out.

"As we see it—and that means me and every member of the executive committee—the problem is that over the years as we've grown in size and become more and more successful, the company gradually has gotten more and more rigid and compartmentalized. Thinking patterns have become fixed. Processes have gotten overcomplicated. We've focused more and more on internal objectives and departmental goals and less and less on our products and our customers. So that today, the organization often works against us, not for us."

"This is startling news," whispered Kate, sarcastically.

"It is to some people," I said. I watched Dick Eggart shift anxiously in his seat.

"We all know," continued Ferry, "that rigid, compartmentalized organizations move too slowly to respond to changes in the marketplace. We know all too well the processes that generate me-too products. The procedures that reward safe thinking. We can feel how the chains of business-as-usual can slowly

7

wrap an organization up, tighter and tighter, until it must either break free or die."

"Nice metaphor," hissed Kate, "but what does he want us poor slobs to do about it?"

Ferry lowered his tone. "We have a vision of a new FCI. A company focused on three vital concerns. One: creating delightful products. Two: being early to market. Three: working in teams."

He let these three "vitals" sink in for a moment. "Now, you'll be meeting with your managers in the next day or two, and in those meetings you'll be talking more about the first two 'vitals'—Product Delight and Early to Market. So I want to spend a few minutes on the third one, probably the most important—Teamwork."

"Rah-rah," whispered Kate, a little too loudly.

A woman in the row in front of us turned, placed an extended index finger to tightly closed lips, and was about to "shsh" us when she saw that it was Kate behind her. Kate raised one sharp eyebrow and the woman's finger drooped. She managed a weak smile and turned her attention forward again.

"Your first reaction to the word 'teamwork' is probably the same as mine. It's a tired old corporate buzzword that means everything and nothing. How many teams have we all served on? How many programs have we endured that were supposed to reward teamwork but actually rewarded the boss's favorite employee? How many teams have produced real results? But the kind of teamwork we're talking about is different."

The audience leaned collectively forward, anxious to know where this was headed.

"We believe that only by working in teams will we be able to create delightful products and get them to market early enough to be successful. Teamwork, in other words, is crucial to our corporate mission. And, from this day on, I consider a commitment to working in teams as a condition of employment here at FCI."

Ferry walked back to the podium, giving us a few moments to absorb the impact of what he had said. He turned and smiled.

"That's a strong statement, I know. But we're talking about

fundamental changes to the way we work together at FCI. We're talking about creating a flexible, responsive organization that works in teams to swiftly develop delightful products. And we've given this program a change of name. We call it the New World."

"That's original," whispered Kate. I ignored her.

"As I said, every member of the executive committee is committed to building this New World. And now I'm asking each and every one of you to make a commitment to it as well. Because the only way we're going to create real change at FCI— and if we don't change, we won't survive—is to harness every ounce of talent, energy, and resource we have. The New World, in other words, depends on you."

Ferry gazed out over the audience. Silence. He looked down at his notes and straightened them as if tidying his thoughts. He looked up again.

"You'll be hearing a great deal more about specifics over the next few days. We want to hear your thoughts and comments. But for now, let me just say"—the boyish Ferry smile— "welcome to the New World."

2. *Burning Wires.*

Two minutes after the meeting was over, the great communications network of the Fick was on fire. Not since the Purge had there been such intensity of talk around the untold number of water coolers, coffee machines, copiers, and bathroom stalls. The telephone network was under siege. A data storm of E-mail threatened to overwhelm the electronic network. Voice mailboxes overflowed. Fax machines churned.

It always amazed me how quickly we could communicate among the thousands of employees in the hundreds of buildings in the six groups in the fifty-three countries—like the members of Robin's Merry Band, firing a barrage of arrows with unfailing accuracy all over Sherwood.

The questions were phrased in a hundred different ways. . .

"Is this New World thing Ferry's idea?"

"Does the executive committee really support Ferry?"

"Who's on the executive committee anyway?"

"Who came up with the nauseating term, Product Delight?"

"When is Early to Market? Earlier than what?"

"Is this a smokescreen for big layoffs?"

"Are we going to reorganize? Again?"

"Is this a way to cut costs?"

"FCI is *not* in trouble. We're solid as a rock."

"What about the Total Quality teams? Where do they fit in?"

"Where do I hide?"

But they all boiled down to one essential question: "What does this mean to *me*?"

3. *Jasper Brandishes the Gauntlet.*

With a simple ten-minute speech, Bill Ferry had created a whole new atmosphere at FCI. There was electricity in the air, a heightened intensity that was obvious from the moment I pulled my car into the parking lot the next morning. People moved a little more quickly. They seemed more alert. The simple hello's and good morning's from co-workers were pitched a little higher and articulated a little more sharply.

But the energy, as yet, was unfocused and undirected. The excitement and expectation were mixed with worry and uncertainty. Every comment seemed to carry an underlying question: What's really going on? What is going to happen?

At ten o'clock Friday morning, we held our Technology Systems staff meeting as usual—a weekly gathering of the senior program managers (of which I was one) and representatives of the functional departments that reported directly to Jasper Lash, chief of TSG and FCI senior vice-president. The meeting routinely was held in the Rugby Room (all conference rooms at FCI, for some long-forgotten reason, are named for competitive sports) on the fourth floor of Building Three. The typical agenda: Review of sales and program results. New product or program presentations. Sales forecasts and marketing plans. New business.

Motivated, perhaps, by Ferry's exhortation to shake off old patterns, I chose not to sit in my regular seat at the conference table. On an impulse, I slipped into the place normally occupied by Kate Fiersen. As I did so, I felt all eyes in the room dart my way. It was not as if I were doing anything illegal—seats had never been formally assigned—but the deviation from the norm was noticed. Kate sailed into the room a moment later.

"Is this revenge for yesterday?" she asked, pointing a finger at my heart. Before I could answer, Jasper slipped into the room and took his place at the head of the table.

"Let's begin," he said.

Normally Jasper opened the staff meeting with a few minutes of convivial banter. Kate sensed from his abrupt tone that he was not in the mood for delay that morning, and she settled into the chair next to me.

"I expect you want to know more about the New World, before we go on to our regular business," Jasper began. He crisply opened a new, black portfolio and extracted his chunky Mont Blanc pen from an inner pocket. Then he smiled and looked from face to face. Jasper is a small man, quick and sharp in movements and in wit, and always impeccably dressed—usually in a dark double-breasted suit, starched white shirt, and silk madder bow tie. His most distinguishing physical feature is his gleaming bald head.

"Jasper," said Kate abruptly, "can you give us a little background? What's the genesis of this New World program?"

"You mean you'd like me to sort out the politics for you," Jasper said, with a tinge of distaste in his voice. Kate generally based her actions on political concerns, which Jasper disliked, particularly when she sided against him on some issue.

"I'm just trying to understand what's going on, Jasper," Kate said innocently.

"Of course. Well, as you know, Ferry turned the European operation around and he was brought to the U.S. to give us a similar shot in the arm. The executive committee has been in discussions about future directions virtually from the day he arrived and a lot of the talk was about the need for TSG to reassert our leadership in the office systems market. We

11

reached consensus at the executive committee retreat two weeks ago."

This in itself was remarkable. The executive committee was famous for internecine battles over policy and corporate direction. They would issue mission statements and corporate visions and hang them on the wall for nobody to read. Because there was little unity within the committee, we managers found ourselves constantly trying to guess which member had the most influence on any given issue and aligning our programs accordingly. If the members of the executive committee were unanimously supporting the New World, Ferry had already scored an early victory.

Kate pressed Jasper. "But is it a reorganization, a program, or what?"

"It's not a reorganization. We won't be fiddling with group structure or organizational charts. But I think it will become clear—" Jasper swiveled out of his chair and picked up a marker from the whiteboard tray—"if I simply go through the vitals."

He uncapped the marker and tried to write. Instead of ink, a dry, squeaky noise flowed from the pen.

"Damn," said Jasper, capping the marker and tossing it neatly into a nearby wastebasket. "I don't understand why we can't have markers that work around here."

He grabbed another one and everyone was relieved to see that it actually functioned. He wrote PRODUCT DELIGHT in his scrawly hand.

"Now, whether you like the phrase itself is immaterial." He gestured with the marker. "What we mean by *delight* is this. FCI wants to offer products that customers are not just satisfied with, but take delight in. And delight has some clearly defined characteristics."

Jasper turned and scribbled each one on the board as he spoke. "Easy to use. Simple to maintain. Low total cost of ownership, although not necessarily the lowest purchase price. Aesthetic appeal. Functional innovation. And the highest possible content of nontoxic and recyclable materials."

Jasper flipped the marker into the air and caught it. "This is not our normal list of product attributes, I realize. But," said Jasper, suddenly excited, "imagine the possibilities. Try to imagine creating products that people *love*, not just tolerate. That's what we want to do."

He turned back to the board. "Number two," said Jasper. He scrawled EARLY TO MARKET on the board, beneath PRODUCT DELIGHT. "We don't necessarily want to be the first to market. But our goal is to be the first with the best and most innovative product in its category. Ferry made it clear yesterday that being late to market is a major FCI problem. And I think we all would agree."

Jasper exchanged the green marker for a bright orange one. "And how do we accomplish the above?" he asked rhetorically, scrawling TEAMWORK in letters twice as high as the other two phrases.

Jasper recapped the marker, tossed it into the tray, and smiled at us. He waited for someone to ask a question.

Dick Eggart raised a finger. "What do you mean by teamwork? We already have good teamwork."

"New World teamwork has a specific meaning," said Jasper. He grasped the back of his chair and leaned forward to us.

"Ferry has charged the head of each FCI group to form a New World team. The teams will be cross-functional in nature. That means, of course, that they'll be composed of people from a variety of functions and disciplines, as necessary. The teams will report to a special steering committee but will have substantial autonomy. The mission of each team will be to develop a new product—with Product Delight—and bring it Early to Market. Within the next twelve months."

Jasper paused and looked around the table. He chuckled. "Close your mouths, everyone, bugs might fly in." Evidently we were all in open-mouthed shock. Six new products in twelve months? Product Delight? Cross-functional teams? Was this feasible? Was it prudent?

I asked the pivotal question. "Who's going to lead our team?"

"Someone in this room," said Jasper. "Do I have a volunteer?"

Silence. The executive committee members may have made their verbal commitment to Ferry, but now Jasper was asking for something far more than mere commitment from one of us. He was looking for a neck-on-the-line, ass-bare-to-the-breeze martyr. Our instincts, our experience, everything we knew about the great whirlpool of politics, career jockeying, deal making, and favor trading that constituted life and ensured success at FCI told us *do not volunteer for this one.* No movement was perceptible around the table. Not a blink. Not a shoulder shift. Not a leg crossing.

"We don't have to identify the team leader at this meeting," said Jasper. "But I want to do so by the end of the week. Now, you must have a lot of questions."

We had nothing but questions, but it all seemed so broad and ambitious and so out of the standard Fickie operating procedure that for a moment, no one could speak. I broke the silence.

"What criteria are you going to use to choose the team leader?"

"Good question," said Jasper. "The most important criterion is that the team leader must be committed to making this work. Seriously and genuinely. If you're looking for brownie points or a way to create a bigger power base or control a bigger budget, or if you want to unload some project you're currently working on, forget it. That's not what this is about."

"What about skills?" I asked.

"Anyone in this room has the necessary skills to be the team leader," said Jasper. "Of course, you'll have to go through some basic training. But the best person for the job is the one who can inspire and motivate a group of people with diverse skills and priorities and get them to produce results. We're not looking for drill sergeants or cowboys. A cross-functional team leader is not a traditional boss. This is about sharing responsibility and decision making and focusing on the task."

Dick Eggart held up a cautious finger again. "Who will the team leader report to, and what about compensation? Is there a bonus involved?"

Jasper hated to repeat anything he thought had already been made clear. "As I said, Dick, the team leader reports to me, but enjoys a lot of autonomy. He or she will be highly empowered, as the current phrase would have it. As far as compensation, the team leader will continue at current salary level until his or her next regular review."

"But what about, you know, career path and promotions? Where does team leader fit on the org chart?"

"That's the point, Dick," said Jasper. "If you listened to what Ferry was saying, it was that we're trying to loosen the org chart up a bit."

"But what about the people who have spent years working their way up through the organization? Are you saying that seniority and service don't count for anything any more? That's not fair, is it?" Dick, the Fickie lifer, had always imagined himself as CFO one day and didn't want anything to disrupt that vision or the route he had chosen to achieve it.

"No, we're not saying that," Jasper reassured him. "We're saying that teamwork is now a condition of employment, but that doesn't mean the team leaders are going to knock everybody else out of the organization. After all, we're talking about only six people to start, one from each group."

Dick was not yet reassured. "But how are these New World teams different from the quality teams we already have?"

"The quality teams are more project oriented," said Jasper, "and tend to be within functions. The New World teams are going to be cross-functional, more focused on the broad process of new-product development. They don't replace the quality teams."

"What if you don't get a volunteer for team leader?" Kate asked.

Jasper shrugged. "I'll simply tell the steering committee that no one in TSG is willing to take the risk and we don't field a team. I'm not going to force anybody into this."

"Have any of the other groups formed teams yet?" I asked.

"C&P has," said Jasper, referring to the Consumables & Peripherals Group, the most profitable and fastest-growing group in the company. "I don't know about the others, but I will by tomorrow."

Silence. "I should say," said Jasper, "that if no one of you volunteers, I don't intend to give up. I will simply cast my net wider within TSG. There are several talented, hungry young managers who might jump at the chance."

Another silence. Jasper had thrown down the gauntlet. He checked his watch. "I think we really should get on to our regular business before we get kicked out of this room."

The meeting continued for another hour. The words of our presentations were measured and the whirr of the overhead projector was soothing, but, beneath the calm, it was clear that the ground at FCI was shifting. We all felt unsteady on our feet.

4. *I Ponder My Situation.*

I sat in my beloved, ergonomically designed executive chair (the one I had foraged from an empty office the first week I arrived at FCI) and rolled it from one side of the plastic carpet protector to the other and back again. From my window I could see the duck pond, the running trails, the close-cut lawn of the multiacre Fickie campus, and the prominences of the little town beyond.

Looking out that window, and remembering how hard I had worked to ascend to this fifth-floor office, I wondered why I was even considering volunteering for team leader. My job was secure, at least as secure as a job ever is. I had a high level of responsibility. I was well compensated. Why venture outside the boundaries? Wouldn't the risks outweigh the benefits?

And yet I knew that my job, as it was, wasn't satisfying enough. I had more to contribute. I wanted to take on more responsibility. But would this team business be the right avenue for me? It could as easily be a dead end.

While musing, I idly shuffled through the day's stack of mail. At the bottom I came to the latest issue of *Fortune*. The cover featured a bold headline, CAPTAIN COURAGEOUS, superimposed over a full-page photograph of a corporate chieftain at the helm of an oceangoing yacht. His hands rested steadily on the burnished titanium wheel, and his bright eyes were fixed on the distant horizon. The subheadline read, "MarTech's J. Sanford Picker Charts a Bold Course."

I snapped to attention. J. Sanford Picker. Sandy Picker! I knew this courageous captain of industry—it was the same Sandy Picker I had gone to school with. The same arrogant brass-ring grabber who had come to class each day wearing a pair of dilapidated, two-tone boat shoes identical to those in the cover photograph.

And old Sandy Picker was now the Captain. I was not. He

was Courageous. I was not. He was on the cover of *Fortune*. I tried to imagine what headline the editors could bestow on me. All I could come up with was NICE SMART GUY PLODS ALONG.

That miserable vision made my decision for me.

On my way out the door I nearly collided with Andrea, marketing specialist and my general administrative assistant. In her late twenties, Andrea is a woman of intense clarity. Dark eyes, dark, short-cut hair, swift and elegant gestures. She had been out of the office for a couple of days on business, and so had missed the advent of the New World.

"Ron, have you got a minute?"

"Not right now. I've got to see Jasper."

"What about?" Andrea and I generally knew each other's activities, and none of our current projects required a visit with Jasper.

"I'm going to volunteer. Captain Courageous. The New World," I babbled.

Andrea shook her head as if her hearing had failed.

"Excuse me?"

"I'll explain later. I've got to get up there now. One of those hungry young ones might get in before me."

"What?"

I knew I wasn't making any sense, but I was seized with a tremendous sense of urgency.

"I'll talk to you later, Andrea. Soon as I finish with Jasper." I rushed past her.

Andrea called after me. "Ron, what is going on!"

5. *I Take Courage.*

I knocked at the half-opened door of Jasper's corner office. One floor up from mine and one floor down from Ferry's.

"Ron, come in," Jasper greeted me. "I hope you're here for what I think you're here for."

He closed the door behind me, gestured at me to sit on his couch, and punched the do-not-disturb code into his phone.

I was already feeling the rush of commitment beginning to subside. "I just wanted to discuss it a little further."

17

"Of course." Jasper perched on the leather chair opposite and looked down on me. "What do you want to know?"

What did I want to know? I wanted to know that it would work and be all right. That there was no risk. That I would not fail.

"How serious is this?" I asked instead.

Jasper interlaced his fingers and bent his knuckles back. "Very. Ferry's intent on creating fundamental change."

"How do we know it's going to work?"

"We don't. But Ferry has done it before and been success-ful. And so have plenty of other companies. As I'm sure you know."

"Who's on the steering committee?"

"The six group chiefs. Ferry. Senior people from R&D, sales and marketing, manufacturing, finance, human re-sources, and customer service."

He named them all. It was a group of heavyweights.

"So you're convinced this is a real thing?" I asked.

"Absolutely."

"What about the product? Have you identified the product yet?"

"No. But we have a couple of candidates."

"Which are?"

"FlyingFox is an intriguing possibility. It fits the market we want to be in. All the research is promising."

All development projects at FCI are code named with a word beginning with *F*. No one is quite sure why, but we sus-pect the tradition began with Dr. Osgood. I had heard the code name FlyingFox but couldn't remember any details about the project.

"But the selection of project is entirely up to you. So long as it fits with our overall TSG strategy—to regain dominance in office systems."

I had not expected this. Being able to select the product was an exciting prospect, for the choice could have a genuine impact on the fortunes of the company. Positively or nega-tively.

"What about the team members?" I continued.

"Recruitment is your responsibility."

"Any restrictions?"

"You can't commandeer them. I won't order anybody to join. You have to get the cooperation of each recruit's manager. You need to represent the key disciplines. But you can recruit anybody you think you need within those guidelines."

Jasper was throwing the corporation open before me and challenging me to get the best out of it.

"I still report to you?"

"I know it's a hardship, Ron." Jasper grimaced in mock suffering. "But, yes, you would report to me. Informally. I don't expect laborious written reports. I do expect to be kept informed of major decisions before they're final. What's your product? Why? Who are the team members? What's your schedule? What are your forecasts? What's your manufacturing plan, your marketing plan? How do you plan to spend your budget?"

"How about the steering committee?"

"The steering committee meets twice a month. I'll keep them informed of your progress. There will be two formal presentation and approval stages. First, in about two months, you make a presentation to get program approval. Second, about five or six months later, you go for production approval."

"So, the project could be killed at either of those stages."

Jasper clapped his hands together. "Yes. It could."

"Has anybody else volunteered from our group?"

"Nope," said Jasper, shrugging his shoulders, as if the nonvolunteers were missing a great opportunity.

"What about the other divisions? Have they selected their team leaders yet?"

"What difference does it make?" asked Jasper. "Ron, I'm not asking you to join a volleyball team. I'm asking you to stick your neck out. To make a bold move. I don't care if nobody else in the company forms a team, we're going to go forward anyway."

Jasper, in a strange tribute to his perfectly shaped, gleaming dome, collects baldness artifacts. The centerpiece of his collection, which he calls "All Things Bald," is a wooden phrenologist's head. It was currently in the position of honor on the coffee table between us. Jasper poked his finger at the zone marked COURAGE.

"This is going to take courage, Ron. It is not going to be easy. But I think it will be worth the effort."

"What if I screw it up? What if the team can't pull it off?" I asked.

Jasper pursed his lips. "All I can tell you is that our goal is to do everything we can to help you succeed. My neck is on the line, too."

"And what if we succeed? What happens *after* we get a good product to market? How is that going to affect my position? My compensation?"

"Your performance will be evaluated in the context of the team. If the team succeeds, you succeed. But teams evolve and responsibilities change. I can't tell you exactly how things will look two years from now. All I can tell you is that this is the way the company's going—the way *most* companies are going. I suspect you'll be better off as team leader than as program manager."

I hesitated. Jasper sensed that I was teetering.

"Ron," he said, "I think you're the very best person for this job. I was hoping it would be you knocking at my door. If you hadn't, I was going to knock on yours."

"Why?" I asked.

Jasper raised his eyebrows. "You have all the requisite skills. You understand our products. You have good people management skills."

I thought of Andrea and wondered.

"You've got a lot of energy. Good credibility. You present well. You roll with the punches."

"This is flattering, Jasper, but there are at least two or three others I can think of who are at least as wonderful as I am."

"Yes. But you have one other crucial attribute."

"Which is?"

"You care."

I snorted. But I had already made up my mind. There was only one question left. "What do I do first?"

Jasper tossed his phrenology skull up in the air and caught it playfully. "The training course starts on Tuesday."

It was past five when Jasper and I finished. I decided that since I would be entering the New World on Monday, there was no sense in hanging around the Old World any longer that evening. In a daze, I returned to my office to pick up my briefcase. As I passed Andrea's cubicle, she pounced on me.

"You didn't do what I think you just did, did you?" she demanded.

"What do you think I did?"

"Volunteered to be team leader of the TSG New World team."

"You've been doing some research in the past half hour."

"Since no one around here tells anybody anything, you have to find out for yourself."

This was not quite true, but Andrea was upset, and when she was upset she was prone to exaggeration.

"Why didn't you discuss this with me before you volunteered?"

"I guess I didn't think it was really your issue."

"But it's going to affect me, isn't it? I mean, if you become the team leader, what about the program group we have already?" she asked. "Are we still a team?

"Probably yes."

"And what about me? If you're the team leader, am I automatically a team member? And who decides?"

"Do you want to join?"

"I don't even know what the team is supposed to do yet. How am I supposed to decide?"

"I can tell you what the mission is."

"But what about all our other projects? We have too much work to do already. How are we going to get it all done?"

"We may have to put some projects on the back burner. Hand off a few assignments to other people. We may have to hire somebody new."

She bristled. "Another marketing specialist, you mean?"

"I haven't thought that through yet, Andrea."

"And how long is this team supposed to last? Is it permanent? Is it a task force? Is it a committee?"

"It will last for at least a year, if the product we choose is approved. After that, I don't know."

Andrea sighed. I checked my watch.

"I have to get home, Andrea. Child duty. Can we talk about this more tomorrow?"

"Tomorrow is Saturday."

I started to shuffle homework into my briefcase and grabbed my suit jacket. "I'll call you over the weekend, then," I said.

"I'll be away tomorrow. Call me Sunday, will you?"

"Where are you going?"

"Mark and I are going on a bike trip." Mark was her current boyfriend.

"Have fun."

She looked out the window and nervously tapped her fingernail against my desk. "How can I have fun if I spend the whole weekend worrying about my job?"

I didn't know how to reassure her.

"Don't worry," I said. "I'll call you."

6. Family Counsel.

I drove home slowly, my mind crowded with disconnected thoughts, currents of excitement and eagerness, fulgurations of doubt. The prospect of success I probably could handle, even if it didn't land me on the cover of *Fortune*. But what if we didn't succeed? I had brought new products to market before, but they always had been company initiatives. I never had operated under this kind of pressure or with such a high profile. I decided that I had to proceed under the assumption that failure would mean the end of my career at FCI. Failure in a noble effort was a respectable prospect.

But what if the New World was just a whim of an eager new CEO? How many corporate initiatives and programs that were "really serious" had we all signed on to, only to watch them be abolished or abandoned. It was likely that I could take on the job of team leader, then watch the New World fizzle around me and end up neither a courageous captain nor a noble failure.

A small Post-it note was stuck to the kitchen cabinet. "Ron. At a meeting. Please feed kids. Janice." A survey of the refrigerator led me to the conclusion that, unlike Jasper, Janice had not provided the resources necessary to back up my role as dinner provider. I hastily devised an action plan that called for the use of an outside supplier, Pizza Pallazzo.

There was a burst of physical and vocal energy at the back door. It was child number 1, Kip (ten years old), and two neighbor boys, followed by child number 2, Emma (age six).

"Hi kids."

"Dad, Mum isn't home. We're going to have dinner next door." Kip started to lead everybody back out again.

"We're going to get pizza for dinner," I said.

"No, thanks," said Kip. "Come on, everybody."

"I'll go with you, Dad," said Emma.

"Wait a minute!" I called, following Kip halfway down the hall.

The door slammed. I looked back at Emma, but discovered that she, too, had vanished.

"Emma!"

Water suddenly thundered from the upstairs bathroom.

"Emma?!"

"I can't hear you. I'm taking a bath!" she screamed.

I was asleep by the time Janice got home. Next morning, before she or Emma awoke, Kip and I went off to our first soccer practice of the season. Our team, the Tibias (named for the large shinbone so crucial to soccer success), had several new kids, and I knew it would be an uphill battle to get them playing effectively together. That morning, as I struggled to get the kids to pass the ball to each other, golf seemed an attractive alternative.

It wasn't until Sunday afternoon that I had a chance to talk with Janice about the New World.

"It sounds like a suicide mission to me," she said. "Has anybody else volunteered?"

"I don't know yet," I said. "Why?"

"If they're all whiners and fringe types, the whole thing will have no credibility."

"Am I a whiner?"

"Of course not. But you haven't been very satisfied recently, have you?"

"Maybe not."

"What about resources?"

"Jasper says the board has allocated substantial resources for the New World."

"Enough to fund all six projects?"

"I don't know."

"I'd be willing to bet they'll kill one or two projects because there won't be enough resources to go around."

"I didn't get that impression," I said. "I think the money is there."

"Okay, but what about people and facilities? Your people are going to have a lot of demands on them."

"True." I was thinking that it would have been nice if Janice had begun this interrogation with at least a small word of congratulation.

"But it could be very exciting, Ron," she said, reading my thoughts. "I mean, I have no doubt you can pull it off. Do you?"

"Of course I do."

"Do you get more money?"

"No. Not at the moment."

Janice raised her eyebrows. "Do you get a promotion?"

"No. I get . . ." I paused. "I suppose I get a chance to make a real difference."

She nodded. "That's important." She reached for the front page of the Sunday paper. "I just hope you don't get fired."

That night I had a disturbing dream. I was walking past a newsstand on a crowded downtown street and I saw from a distance that it was entirely stocked with copies of *Fortune*. As I got closer I could see that it was me on the cover. Smiling. Confident.

And naked.

7. *The Martha Model.*

The dream haunted me Monday morning as I drove to work. It seemed to me that although I had always considered myself an effective manager and team player, I really had spent my entire career trying to advance *myself*. Perhaps I wasn't ruthless like J. Sanford Picker, but I had little idea how to go about building, motivating, or managing a cross-functional team. I didn't have the skills or the knowledge, hadn't been able to answer Andrea's most basic questions about the team. I realized I needed to talk with someone at my own level, someone who had experience with teams and could serve as a neutral and objective adviser. Someone who was not Jasper.

Martha Morgan, head of the consumables & peripherals group, came to mind. C&P was a profitable but glamourless FCI salt mine, where thousands of quotidian items, supplies, and components were sold directly to customers through catalog and telephone sales. Before Martha, only the dullest of Fickies toiled at C&P. It was the Siberia to which you were assigned if you couldn't be fired.

Then, during the Purge, Martha took over as C&P chief. With tremendous energy, she transformed the operation. Within eight months, the most ambitious Fickies were scratching and clawing each other to get in. People who had never laid eyes on a customer before became obsessed with customer service. People who had never heard of continuous improvement fretted endlessly about Total Quality and how to achieve it.

C&P became a cult. They reveled in chanting their toll-free number at Friday beer parties. Their chests swelled with pride when they talked about their same-day turnaround. Their success had become the subject of several magazine articles (although no *Fortune* covers) and was often cited by FCI senior executives. From an outsider's perspective it seemed that Martha's group exemplified successful teamwork.

C&P was headquartered in the original home of FCI, affectionately referred to as the Garage—a large, two-story, brick carriage house. Martha met me at the double glass doors that had replaced the original wooden ones and escorted me into an atmosphere markedly different from that I had encountered anywhere in FCI Buildings One through Five. The place was full of energy. There was laughter. It was difficult to tell the managers from the managed.

"What's everybody so excited about?" I asked Martha. "Is this the result of teamwork? Sixty grown-ups acting happy?"

Martha laughed. "I suppose it is. We happen to love the stuff we sell. We like helping our customers. We're totally focused on getting the order right and getting it out on time."

Martha's office was on the mezzanine level, a large space with floor-to-ceiling windows that looked out over the cubicles below; her floor was strewn with samples of C&P products.

"But your mission is different from ours, Ron." She tucked one ankle beneath the opposite knee. Martha is a calm, soft woman who favors office-styled exercise clothing. "We're a different kind of team from the one you're going to put together."

"In what way?"

"The C&P team is a natural work group. The core group of people who make up our team work together as a part of their regular responsibilities. We're essentially a single-function team—all customer service people. We're in the same physical location and we speak the same business language. I don't have to deal with salespeople trying to communicate with, let's say, programmers."

"So you don't have experience in building cross-functional teams?"

"Sure. We form ad hoc teams or task forces to address a particular problem or implement a specific something or other. We might have a manufacturing person involved, or an engineer, or a shipping and distribution guy, so they're usually cross-functional. Plus, C&P'ers are involved in long-range teams, similar to the New World steering committee."

"Do you have any advice for me? How do you suggest I go at this?"

Martha took a sip from a large tumbler of water that appeared to be a fixture of her working life.

"You are going to get some training, aren't you, Ron?"

"Starting tomorrow."

"You'll get a lot of help with the basics, then. So maybe the best thing I can do is talk about the big issues."

"Please."

"The number-one issue is getting commitment and support from your managers. You won't get anywhere unless Jasper and Ferry back you up. And it sounds as if they do."

"They certainly say they do."

"They should let you run your own show and not bog you down with a lot of reports and presentations and approval cycles."

"Jasper's talking about two formal presentations to the steering committee. The rest would be informal."

"Good. Number two. Is your mission well defined? Is it clear what they're asking you to do?"

"Frighteningly so."

"You mean you don't think the objective is achievable?"

"Difficult. But achievable."

"Okay. Another issue is resources. You can gauge the support you're getting when you request money, or people, or equipment."

"We haven't reached that point yet."

"Time, too. If Jasper and Ferry or the steering committee aren't willing to give you enough time, if they're not accessible, that's a clear signal. Make sure you get the time you need from them."

"What about evaluation? Dick Eggart is already fretting about his career track and Andrea is worried I'm going to hire a new person to compete with her."

"Those are legitimate issues. The team members have to understand what their team responsibilities are going to be and the performance criteria on which you're going to evaluate them."

"Ferry has said that teamwork is a condition of continued employment here at FCI."

"Sure," said Martha. "But nobody really knows what that means yet, specifically. Some functional managers are going to consider team membership as an extracurricular activity, like field hockey. It's nice for their people, but it's not absolutely necessary. And some managers are going to think of team responsibilities as getting in the way of the person's *real* work."

"There are going to be a lot of conflicting demands on my team members, I suppose."

"That's why you want to be careful who you choose to join the team. If someone isn't committed, when the pressure gets too great, they'll just cave in. Have you thought about which disciplines will be represented on your team?"

"R&D. Engineering. Manufacturing. Marketing communications. Probably sales. Maybe finance. My strength is in marketing."

"Think of the differences in those kinds of people. You're talking about bringing together people from rival kingdoms and alien culture zones and asking them to collaborate. Just think of the labels we pin on each other."

At FCI, the dominant professional types were often referred to as air breathers (marketing), propellor heads (technical), bean counters (finance), and 40,000 footers (senior managers and frequent flyers).

"You're talking about deep and long-standing prejudices and animosities," Martha said. "And, as organizationally correct as you think you are, Ron, I guarantee that you've got some prejudices of your own."

"I expect I do," I said, convinced that I didn't.

"And those conflicts are not going to go away immediately. They may never go away. But your job is not to change people's souls, it's to get them working together effectively. And you can't do that without their commitment. Remember, people join teams for all kinds of reasons. They may say they're committed, but just because they show up for your meetings doesn't mean their hearts are really with the team."

"I suppose not."

"You've got another challenge with your mission." Martha took a slug of water. "It's clear to us at C&P if we're meeting our objectives. We can measure our percentage of on-time delivery. The number of back orders. Things like that. But a significant part of the product development process you're going to be involved in is creative. Your key measurement doesn't come until the end of your process, when the product goes to market. You won't ultimately know if you're successful until the product sells."

"There's not much I can do about that."

"Sure there is. You can establish achievable goals along the way. A team needs early success to get the juices flowing, make them feel like the process is fun."

"Such as?"

"Getting approval at the two presentations you mentioned are the formal ones. Focus on those."

"Okay," I said, scribbling some notes.

"That reminds me." Martha rummaged through a basket on her desk and plucked out a computer disk. "These are notes I've made over the past couple of years, then edited and refined. You might want to incorporate them into your teamwork file."

"Thanks." I tucked the disk into my briefcase. I didn't yet have a teamwork file, but I resolved to create one.

"Martha, excuse me." A young woman poked her head in the door. "Are you going to join us?"

Martha checked her watch. "Why don't you go and get started and I'll be there in a few minutes." The woman nodded and hurried off.

Martha explained. "Today is our first C&P New World team meeting."

"But you don't have any products per se, do you? What will your team be working on?"

"Our services are our products, and there's always a new way to improve our service to the customer."

I wondered whether Martha could be an effective adviser for me if she also was working with her own group's team. As large as FCI is, it is virtually impossible to find anybody inside who can be truly impartial, who is agendaless and has no ax to grind. But Martha came as close as anyone.

"What else?" Martha continued. "Oh, yes, communications. Your team members are not going to be in contact every day. You're in Building Three. Engineering's in Building Four. Manufacturing is way out at North River. You may have some outside suppliers in who-knows-where. And maybe you'll need to get some Fickies involved from other U.S. divisions, or from overseas."

"That doesn't worry me. That's just travel."

"Yes," said Martha, taking another sip of water, the ice cubes bumping noisily against the green plastic. "But it's one thing for you to travel as a manager and keep in touch with home base. It's different when there is no home base and *everybody* is traveling."

"I suppose."

Martha shoveled papers into a file folder. "I'll walk you over," she said. "My meeting is in Building Four."

The day had turned gray and flat by the time we emerged from the Garage. I did not feel encouraged.

"You know what I've found about team leading, Ron?"

"Men are no good at it."

Martha looked at me as if I were a dinosaur. "No, I think it's a skill that has nothing to do with gender."

"Just kidding," I said, feeling foolish.

"What I've found is that most of the problems get much easier to solve once you make the fundamental adjustment."

"What is that?"

"That *you* will have to change. You, Ron Delaney, as effective and successful and talented and charming as you are, will have to change. You're going to have to manage in a new way. The old ways that made you so effective and successful won't work in the New World. Do you know what I mean?"

"I think so."

"You *will* think so. When you get done with the training course, you'll think, 'Oh, this is just common sense. Nothing to it. I know all this stuff already.' But knowing the basics intellectually is a different thing from putting them into practice."

"But when you say I have to change, what do you mean? In what way?"

We had reached an intersection where one paved path led to Building Three, another to Building Four. I stopped and glanced back at the Garage. I could almost hear the phones burring there and the C&P'ers happily filling customer orders.

"You're going to have to change that mental image you have of authority," she said. "You're not being asked to command this team. You're being asked to help your people. Facilitate their jobs. Coach them. Support them. You're not used to that."

The village of new six-story FCI buildings that towered above us looked like a fortress. The image of Captain Courageous, J. Sanford Picker, came to mind. Was he part of the Old World or part of the New? What about me?

"Do you mind if I call you from time to time, Martha?" I asked.

"Of course not, Ron," she said. "Feel free."

On my way back to my office I stopped by the FCI corporate library, which sprawls across a sunlit central atrium in the Old Building. Here, at any hour on virtually any day, you can find information-hungry Fickies staring into computer screens at digitally stored data—text, photographs, music, numbers, even movie and video clips—or lounging in fat green chairs leafing through books, magazines, and newspapers on virtually any subject, from every corner of the world.

After a half hour of inspired rummaging, I had collected a few business classics that I hadn't looked at in years, including *My Years with General Motors,* by Alfred P. Sloan, Jr. (1963), and a personal favorite, *Ragged Dick,* by Horatio Alger (1868). Also a number of current books that I thought might shed some light on my upcoming odyssey. *The Corporation of the 1990s, The Fifth Discipline, Survival of the Fittest,* and *Rethinking the Corporation: The Architecture of Change.*

I returned to my office, stacked the reading material on the credenza, and checked through my E-mail messages.

To: Ron
From: Andrea

You forgot to call me on Sunday! What's happening? Don't forget, I'm out of the office until Thursday with agency reviews, and a personal day—I'm moving into the new apartment. But please leave me a message about this team thing. The suspense is shortening my life expectancy.

To: Andrea
From: Ron

Sorry I forgot to call. I'm out Tuesday and Wednesday on a training course, so let's plan to meet on Friday to discuss it. Don't worry, recent surveys show that average female life expectancy has increased to 82.6 years. Even if you lose two or three years due to suspense, you'll still be long gone from here by the time you pass on.

I opened a new file and made some jottings from my meeting with Martha:

- Team membership is not an extracurricular activity. (Team participation does not equal field hockey.)
- Teams cut across rival kingdoms. Culture clashes are inevitable.
- Team needs some early successes to generate enthusiasm, make people feel the team can succeed.
- Communications are crucial.
- My view of leadership must change. (Hmmm. What is my view of leadership?)

31

8. *I Am Exposed to the Basics and Meet My Fellow Leaders.*

I was not relishing being sequestered with my fellow New World team leaders and undergoing two days of basic training, despite the fact that I knew I needed it. Although I came up with all kinds of rationalizations for my reluctance to attend, my primary concern was that I would be exposed as a novice, or worse. Jasper had made it clear, however, that the training was not optional.

We were assigned to the largest room at the FCI Education Center, known as the Boards. It's about the size of a basketball court, with large windows set high in the walls, allowing in a great deal of sunlight without affording a distracting view. The first person I met when I entered the room was Dick Eggart. He greeted me with exaggerated heartiness.

"Hey, Ron!"

"Dick, what are you doing here?" I hoped to avoid discussion of the forecast numbers I had promised him.

"I'm a New World team leader, of course."

"You're what?" Although Dick sat in on our TSG staff meetings, he was officially an employee of the corporate finance department. "You mean corporate is fielding a New World team?"

"That's right. And I volunteered to run it. I mean lead it."

This was not behavior I would have expected from Dick.

"Doesn't seem like your style, Dick."

Dick lowered his voice. "Listen, Ron. I'm picking up information that when Ferry was in Europe the team leaders were on the fast track for promotion. The really successful ones even leapfrogged some of the senior managers. I don't want that to happen to me."

"Sounds like you're playing the Old World game using New World rules, Dick."

Dick winked as if I had paid him a compliment. "You got to do what you got to do."

Seven teams now, I thought. Fewer resources to go around. And one team leader has his hands on the money. Dick's presence worried me. Perhaps the New World was just another political program after all?

32

"Good morning, team leaders!" The trainer called us to order and my doubts were eclipsed by my apprehensions about what would come next.

During the first hour, we introduced ourselves to each other and talked about the nature and function of teams in general. The team leaders represented a cross section of Fickie life. There was me, the marketing air breather. Dick, the bean counter. The C&P leader. We also had two propellor heads (one man, one woman), a manufacturing jock, and a second marketing type (a woman). Then there were the two trainers from an outside consultancy, and two people from human resources. Eleven people in all.

I did not make a fool of myself. I found that I was neither the star of the class nor the dunce. At Martha's suggestion (reinforced by the trainers), I took copious notes, which I intended to incorporate into my electronic team file as soon as I got the chance. A few of my scribblings:

Role of team leader:
- Goal setter for team, based on corporate goals. (Establish with sponsor.)
- Define responsibilities for each team member. (Talk to Andrea.)
- Communications center. Resolve conflicts with other managers.
- Keeper of team records and information. (Note: delegate this one.)
- Takes on assignments. (Me a worker bee?)
- Recognizes achievement. Rewards.
- Provides measurement/benchmarks.
- Sets ground rules for team. What is expected—meeting attendance, attitude, etc.
- Team champion with senior management.

Over the next two days, we explored every aspect of teamwork: the phases of teams (forming, storming, norming, performing); the objections to joining teams (I would hear some of those in the next few days); problems of teams (lack of trust, unclear objectives, hidden agendas); how to run effective meetings; measuring and rewarding team performance.

By the end of the course, I felt the way a recent college graduate should feel—equipped and energized, ready to go out and build the most potent and successful team in all of corporate history.

9. *I Venture Into the Fiefdom of R&D.*

At FCI, the research and development function has long enjoyed the mantle of corporate glory. Dr. Osgood was an engineer, and he loved to hire the best engineers, nurture them, stimulate their imaginations, stroke their egos, and reward their efforts. As a result, R&D became more a state of mind than a department. We spent millions on it each year. We reveled in the thousands upon thousands of patents we had been awarded over the decades.

In the past few years, however, only the most courageous managers had dared to negotiate the tempestuous waters of R&D. Too many ships had been caught in violent crosscurrents of conflicting priorities, or pushed back by strong headwinds of resistance to change. Yes, FCI's technology advances still made regular headlines. But the stories generally ended with a disclaimer, something like "Practical application of the new discovery, say FCI scientists, is still years away." Some Fickie managers held the view that R&D had become an end in itself, consumed in exploring ever more arcane and specialized topics.

My theory, however, was that it was not the people who were at fault, but the organization. The approval processes for new ideas had become hopelessly complex, involving dozens of functional managers, senior execs, legal and regulatory people. And then there was the inhibiting influence of the dreaded Dr. Emil Zanoski himself, twenty-year Fick veteran and chief of R&D, who presided over the rigorous review and release process with an iron hand.

The fourth-floor lab in Building Four (known as Foursquared) is the heart of R&D for Technology Systems Group. After being buzzed through the pebble-glass door by a disinterested security guard, I negotiated my way among the United Nations of technicians and engineers from Europe, Australia, Japan, Korea, and Latin America who were tinkering at their benches surrounded by breadboards, tangles of wire, testing equipment, soldering guns, ovens, meters, computer terminals, and unidentifiable black boxes.

I located Nick Yu in a corner cubicle not more than six feet square, completely surrounded by computer screens and test boards. Wires ran across his lap and around his ankles. Reams of computer printouts were stacked on his desk, some of them tumbling in folds to the linoleum floor.

"Hello, Nick."

I was only three feet from him, but he didn't hear me. He continued to stare at his monitor and whisper to himself in his native Korean. Finally, I touched him on the shoulder. He leaped out of the chair and came down facing me.

"Ah, Ron!"

"Sorry, Nick. Didn't mean to surprise you." Nick is a small man, not much over thirty years old, with what looks to be about a fifty-fifty blend of Asian and American features. We had worked together on a project the year before, and I had been impressed by both his talent and his flexibility. He loved his work. Plus, he was the current project manager for FlyingFox.

"Ron!" Nick exclaimed again, as if really seeing me this time. "Come in! Sit down!" Without hesitation, he swept a board and computer printout off the only available chair. I reflexively moved to catch the board before it hit the floor, but failed.

"Just trying to preserve the corporate assets," I said, feebly.

"It's worthless," Nick scoffed. "Just an old test board."

"What are you working on?"

"This is a Zanoski project. We need to convert some data from an FEA program that the guys on the West Coast are running and we're having some porting problems, which I think are mostly to do with—"

Nick stopped. "Oh." He held up a hand in apology. "Sorry."

"It's okay." Although I took a couple of engineering courses as an undergraduate, I quickly get lost in the technical jargon.

"What can I do for you?" asked Nick.

"You know about the New World teams," I began.

"You're the TSG leader, right?"

"Yes. And one of my first tasks is to identify our product."

Nick grabbed my shoulders.

"FlyingFox!" he whispered, as if I were his savior. "FlyingFox fits all the criteria of Product Delight. And we can get it to market early. I know we can."

I was impressed at how quickly Ferry's three "vitals" were taking hold throughout the organization. Nick's enthusiasm was so infectious, I found it difficult to be analytical.

"Tell me about it," I said.

"I'll show it to you," said Nick. He snatched up his coat, took me by the arm, and virtually dragged me out of his cubicle.

Nick led me down the back stairs and pushed through a heavy steel door into a sunless, airless basement laboratory. He guided me past another set of workbenches and another set of engineers, down a long linoleum corridor to a second steel door with no markings. He shoved it open and we entered.

There, like a comatose patient on a high-tech operating table, lay FlyingFox. It was a conglomeration of mechanical and electronic components, most of them obviously handmade, held together by a sheet-metal skeleton and laced through with a profusion of multicolored wires.

"What is it?" I asked.

Nick smiled.

"Good morning, FlyingFox," he said, enunciating with exaggerated distinction.

"Good morning," a surprisingly human-sounding voice responded from within the jumble of parts. "You are looking at the next generation of office machine. It will do for printing and copying what the fax machine did for electronic communications. I am now teddy."

"Teddy?" I asked. "What does that mean?"

"Ready. It said *ready*," said Nick. "As in, ready to operate." It had not sounded like *ready* to me, but Nick kept going. "FlyingFox has paper-handling functionalities that are unlike anything on the market. It links easily into any computer network." Nick then spent twenty minutes demonstrating how

36

FlyingFox interfaced with computer-based documents and how paper was processed through its workings.

"It has very few mechanical parts, you see, so it's easy to maintain," said Nick. "It operates by voice response, which is a unique feature. And I'm sure we can design an exterior housing that will have aesthetic appeal."

"What about the recycling issue?"

"FlyingFox uses no toxic elements or chemicals in the process. And we have a big opportunity to create the housing out of a recyclable or reclaimable material."

"Such as?"

Nick shrugged. "I'm not a materials expert. I don't have a specific one in mind. But I do not think it will be a problem."

"How close are you to a working prototype?"

"There are a few bugs in the software. The voice response isn't perfect yet. We haven't done any manufacturing engineering. But all the basics are there. You're looking at it."

I was looking at electronic roadkill. Nick was clearly in love with FlyingFox. Just as clearly, FlyingFox was a long way from the marketplace.

"What about Dr. Zanoski? Does he support FlyingFox?"

Nick twitched. He seemed, within the space of a microsecond, to shrink in size. He turned slightly away from me. The hand resting on FlyingFox went still.

"It's not on the priority list," Nick confessed.

"Ah."

"Does Zanoski have to know?"

"Sooner rather than later."

Nick nodded. "Well, he hasn't reviewed FlyingFox in several months. We've come a long way since he last saw it."

"Do you really believe we can make FlyingFox a viable product and get it to market within a year?"

He brightened. "Yes, Ron. I do. And I'll do everything I can to make it happen."

I looked at the blinking bundle of spare parts. I had to confess I had seen prototypes in far worse shape at this stage of development. I was inclined to pursue it further. Nick agreed to sign on as my R&D team member, but with the understanding that FlyingFox was not a sure thing yet. I needed to get some other opinions.

10. *The Man Who Knew Too Much.*

I wanted to get an engineer on board next, someone with an eye for detail and solid practicality to balance Nick's optimism and creative enthusiasm. David Clair was the perfect person for the job. He had been at FCI for seven years and was known as a solid and steady engineer, with an excellent track record in product development. My feeling was that at age thirty-four, he was on the brink of making a major contribution to the company. If it could be with FlyingFox, so much the better.

I was in the cafeteria (in pursuit of frozen yogurt) when I spotted David sitting alone at a distant corner table. He was reading from a large textbook and sipping soup.

"David. May I join you for a moment?" I asked.

David waited to finish reading his sentence before he looked up. He didn't smile. "Okay," he said, with no hint of welcome.

"I expect you know about the New World teams," I began.

"Yes," he said and returned to his reading.

"I'd like to talk with you about working on my team."

"I'm not really interested," he said, without looking up.

"Can you tell me why?"

"I have a completely full schedule. I don't have any time."

Maybe the product itself would be a lure. "We're considering FlyingFox as the team project."

David rubbed his ear. "That technology doesn't interest me much."

"You don't think it's a viable product?"

David looked at me as if I were trying to trap him.

"I didn't say that. I think it probably is a good product. I just meant that the technologies aren't my specialty."

"Nick Yu needs some help from someone like you in getting FlyingFox to the next stage."

"Nick and I don't work that well together. I doubt it would be a good mix."

He continued reading. This guy was not going to come around. "Is there another engineer you can recommend?"

David looked up and pondered the far wall for a moment. "Yeah," he said. "I think the best guy would be Wes Dunn."

I hadn't considered Wesley, whom I knew well from a variety of projects, because I thought he was too senior. Perhaps a little tired and cynical, as well.

"Why?"

"Wes is a superb engineer." David nodded thoughtfully. "But he has to spend too much of his time these days managing. I think he'd get a kick out of something like FlyingFox. Why don't you ask him?"

"Thanks, David. I might. Sorry to disturb your reading."

David smiled and showed me the cover. "Yeah, *The Effects of High Temperature Processing on Long Chain Polymers*. Exciting stuff."

Wesley Dunn had been with FCI since before there was a Technology Systems Group, before there were groups at all, back when FCI possessed only one product and one building, the Garage. When Wesley joined, Dr. Osgood was still actively involved in conceiving and designing products, and could be found at lunchtime eating his vegetable soup from a Thermos bottle in the corner of the basement lab, talking technology and baseball with his colleagues.

Wesley's office is on the third floor of Building Four, a glass-enclosed silo set nearly in the middle of the open floor, surrounded by a matrix of office spaces created by waist-high partitions, each housing a drafting table, a CAD terminal, or both. Here and there a large plotter or printer is at work, print heads jerkily skittering across the page.

Wesley was not in his office when I arrived, although I had called ahead. However, Wesley is the steadiest and most reliable of Fickies—if not quite as talented, perhaps, as David Clair—and so I waited in his doorway. Soon I saw him approaching from the far side of the enormous room. He moved deliberately, threading his way through the desks and CAD terminals, occasionally slowing his stride for a word with one of his colleagues but always remaining in forward motion. There was no self-importance in the way he progressed through the room, yet you could feel that he, and everyone else there, knew that this was his place.

Wes, in his late forties now, is a good-looking man with wavy brown hair that requires occasional pushing back from his forehead, friendly brown eyes, and a small gap between the two upper front teeth that gives him a boyish quality. He is fastidious about his dress; he rolls his shirt cuffs under, precisely one fold, but still exposing the monogram WRD stitched into the sleeve. His necktie is unwaveringly tied in a Windsor knot, the collar usually loosened to reveal a tuft of dark chest hair. Perhaps most telling, Wes is never to be seen without his employee identification badge, which he clips to the middle button of his shirt. The badge displays a photograph of him looking dour, as well as his employee number, 196.

FCI currently has tens of thousands of employees and, over its thirty-odd years of operation, has employed hundreds of thousands. Each one, no matter how brief his or her halcyon stay, is issued a badge number. Badge numbers below 1000 are rare. Numbers under 100 are virtually nonexistent. Anything in between qualifies the wearer for legendary status. Wesley's 196 is the lowest I know of in the company. To have an under-1000 as a member of the team would be an important signal that I had snared a Fickie of eminence.

Wesley kept walking as he shook my hand, using the grip to both greet me and drag me into his office.

"What do you want?" he asked wearily. He was not being unfriendly, merely direct and efficient.

Wes did not close the door. I sat at his conference table and he sat across from me, waiting for me to start. It is always wise to assume that Wesley knows more about what you are coming to talk about than you do. His information network is formidable and provides him with startlingly accurate and prescient data. People are willing to give him information because he never misuses it or reveals its source, and always provides the best information he can in return.

"I assume this is about the New World thing," he said.

"Yes."

"You want to sign me up?"

"Yes. I do."

"Well," said Wesley slowly, "consider me signed." He looked at me evenly. "Anything else?"

"Do you have any questions about the commitment?"

"Sure," said Wesley. "When are the meetings?"

"Weekly. Wednesday mornings."

"Okay." Wesley nodded slowly. "You're going to get

everybody on board with this thing? Somebody from manufacturing. Somebody from sales. So we don't have people screaming at us too late in the process?"

"And from R&D."

"Oh, yeah, Nick Yu." Proof of the efficacy of Wesley's informants.

"Have you worked with him?"

"Nope," said Wesley shortly. "But I think we can make that box of his go."

"There are some engineering challenges involved. Serious ones."

"Always are," said Wesley. Just a faint touch of a closed-mouth yawn.

Wesley was making me uneasy.

"Are you sure you want to get involved in this?"

The yawn bloomed. "Sure, why not?"

"Does your schedule allow it?"

Wes looked at me seriously for the first time. "Oh, sure it does. After all, I'm not quite as in demand as Dave Clair."

I reminded myself: Assume that Wes knows *everything*.

"Dave recommended you."

"As a good second best?"

"No. He thinks you're a superb engineer who doesn't get to do much hands-on engineering any more."

"David said that?"

"Words to that effect."

"That's true enough."

"Actually, I didn't think you'd be interested in joining this team, Wes. You've got a lot of responsibility as it is."

"Sure," he said. He leaned forward now. "But I could use a challenge. I'm in a little bit of a rut right now. Plus, I haven't got as many family responsibilities as I used to."

Wes had just been divorced after twenty-two years of marriage. His only child was living on her own.

"Sorry to hear about you and Alison."

Wesley shrugged as if it was too complicated to talk about, then changed the subject. "What about Zanoski?"

"What about him?"

"What does he think about FlyingFox?"

Wesley probably knew that FlyingFox was not an R&D priority. Although their styles were different—I thought of Zanoski as an Old World command/control manager and Wesley as a consensus builder—they both worked hard to keep the natural tension between R&D and engineering from flaring into open warfare.

"I don't know at this point. I know he isn't up to date on its current status. I know that I'll have to get his commitment."

"What if he says forget it?"

"I don't think he will."

Wesley persisted. "What if he says no?"

"I'll face that when we come to it," I said firmly. "What I really want to know is, do I have *your* commitment? I don't want you to say yes, show up for the first meeting, and then disappear. I want you to help us make FlyingFox the best product it can be."

He studied his shirt cuffs, then ran thumb and forefinger along the crease. "I'll be as serious about the project as the project is about itself. I'd love nothing more than for FCI to generate some Product Delight." He chuckled at the phrase. "But I don't want to get involved in some marketing-driven scheme that's all about gimmicks and fads and image, and nothing to do with good, solid engineering and design. I've done that, believe me. If I get involved with this thing, I want engineering to have a strong voice in the product, and I want our voice to be heard throughout the whole process. I've seen too many good engineering ideas ruined by manufacturing people whining that they couldn't make it, or by marketing people who couldn't make up their minds what they wanted. Not you, of course, though, Ron."

"Wesley, I'm working to build a team. I'm open to your suggestions and I need your help."

"Here's a suggestion. Get a purchasing person on the team."

This surprised me. "Purchasing?"

"I've seen just as many products ruined by some purchasing screwup. We bust our humps creating detailed specifications for hundreds of materials and hundreds of components and then purchasing goes out and tries to substitute second-rate stuff just to shave a penny or two off the unit price."

"Okay," I said, not at all sure if there was anyone in purchasing who could or would commit to joining a New World team. "Let me see what I can do."

Wesley looked at his watch, an elaborate instrument bristling with knobs and dials, seemingly carved out of a solid hunk of a silvery-white metal.

"Titanium," said Wesley, noticing me noticing his watch. I couldn't tell if he was kidding. "Let me know when the first meeting is." His telephone burred, and Wesley turned to answer it. End of meeting with engineering.

11. *In the Land of TQ.*

I decided to drive out to the North River manufacturing facility rather than book a seat aboard the corporate helicopter. It's a pleasant journey through verdant countryside and it gives me a good twenty minutes of uninterrupted, back-of-mind thought.

I was thinking about my team members. Nick Yu. Young and enthusiastic. Very talented. But maybe too willing to play outside the rules. Wesley. Deeply seasoned, extremely stable. But did he have any engineering fire left, or was he a burned-out organization man now? What about Andrea, would she join? Unknowns: I had promised Wesley I would try for a purchasing person. Did I need someone from finance? I definitely needed a marcomms type. Kate Fiersen had the skills and the drive, but could I work with her? And, finally, manufacturing.

Carlos Garcia is manufacturing manager at North River, one of three FCI plants still operating in the state, a plant that specializes in producing components and assembling products for Technology Systems. Carlos is, in my opinion, one of the most progressive managers at FCI. About four years ago he was wooed away from a major competitor, where he had built a formidable reputation as a Total Quality manufacturing manager. He had completely changed the relationship between his company and its many suppliers, created a clear set of guidelines for manufacture, reduced the number of suppliers qualified to sell to the company, and then worked closely with those suppliers to steadily improve quality. Or so I had been told.

Many Fickies had assumed that Carlos' real assignment at

FCI was to close down North River as swiftly as possible and farm out all our manufacturing to offshore companies and local subcontractors. The feeling was that, given our high wage structure and the access to offshore factories we had through international divisions, FCI could not be competitive in manufacturing at home.

Carlos proved the opposite. He had moved quickly to trim costs and unneeded personnel, and then enlisted all his staff—managers, administrators, hourly workers—to help reengineer the core processes. They identified all kinds of procedures and steps within procedures that were unnecessary, and got rid of them. They shifted and retrained people. Now they had become so efficient and produced goods of such high quality that not only could they handle production of all the FCI products necessary, they often took on work from outside, noncompeting companies. In short, the North River manufacturing facility, like Martha's C&P, was a Fickie bright spot, a model of how Total Quality could transform an operation.

But there was a major difference between the two operations. Unlike C&P, North River received very little recognition within FCI. It was almost as if there were an unwritten taboo about mentioning the place. It was odd and, to my mind, unfair and inexplicable.

"I've assembled my team," Carlos told me when he met me in the North River lobby. "Come on, they're waiting." Carlos bounded forward and I rushed after him. He is a slim, athletic man, known throughout the company for his skill as a softball player. He walks quickly, eats fast (although with remarkable tidiness), and, when in a good mood, is graciously polite. There is always, however, a sense of urgency about him. In conversation, if you pause to find the right word or phrase, you feel that Carlos is restraining himself from supplying it for you. If you ask a question or raise an issue that is not directly relevant to the subject, but of interest, Carlos will politely but quickly get the discussion back on track.

Carlos gestured me into the conference room. There I was greeted by four fresh pads of lined paper, a bowl of mints, two pots of freshly made coffee (one with caffeine, one without), and his two key staff people. Carlos put an arm around my shoulders and introduced me to Nelson Favreau, his chief operations person, and Helen Ostroshnick, his quality director. The introductions were followed by the ceremonial distribution of coffee. A basket of extremely large, gooey buns—Fickie rolls!—was placed center table. Although there was much comment about their size and beauty, no one touched the basket.

"Ron asked if he could come down and meet with us about a new project," began Carlos. "Which I know nothing about, so I'll just turn it over to you, Ron."

All eyes on me. I thought, is this the most buttoned-up group at FCI? Or do they have some agenda I'm not aware of? Perhaps they're not as busy as they're reputed to be? Are they trying to become more visible throughout the company? Is Carlos trying to make me show my hand before I'm ready? Then I thought: Old World thinking. I decided to assume that Carlos wanted to show he was interested, had assembled his best people, and that I should take advantage of it.

"I know this is early for manufacturing to get involved," I said, after briefly reviewing the three New World "vitals." "But that's the whole point of my being here. It's important that you have input into the development of the new product from the very start. I know that you usually work closely with engineering during the development of prototypes and later in the design of manufacturing tooling, but I want to push the concept of design-for-manufacture further than we've ever taken it before."

All three heads nodded—slightly.

"I've already spoken with R&D and engineering, and they've committed to working together with you and others to integrate our efforts throughout the process."

"Sounds good," said Carlos. More nods. But some issue lurked beneath the surface.

"I wanted to come down now, show myself, and see if you have any concerns, issues, needs, suggestions about how we might proceed."

A long silence. Finally Carlos broke it.

"Okay. Let me ask a question." He pulled forward, picked up the sharpened pencil by the waiting pad and made one small, crisp doodle. "First, let me say that I appreciate your coming down here at this stage in the process. We really do appreciate that."

Eager nods.

"But," he said, adding another line to the doodle, "the truth is, we're just a little puzzled."

Nelson and Helen froze. Carlos was about to venture into the land of previously unspoken issues.

"Maybe it's because we're a little isolated from the centers of power up where you are, Ron. But . . . you know about the progress we've made in terms of capacity, productivity, and quality here at North River."

"Of course."

"I think everybody would agree—I mean, everybody does agree whenever we talk—that we've made tremendous improvements."

Vigorous nods around the table. Still no one touched the sticky buns.

"That's what brought me here," I said.

"What puzzles us is why about forty percent of our business these days is coming from non-FCI sources. We know that there is lots of FCI work we could be handling, but it's going out to subcontractors or to our plants overseas."

"Are you sure of that?" I asked. Foolish question. Of course he knew his own plant's business.

An exasperated laugh and a lick of the tongue. "Do you doubt it?" Perhaps it was this edge of confrontation that had prevented Carlos' facility from getting better internal publicity.

"No. I'm just surprised. I would think every project manager would be eager to work with North River."

"That's why we're puzzled, Ron. Case in point. Last month, we were approached about picking up maybe twenty percent of production for a key FanFare subcomponent. We got all excited. We put together a feasibility study. We ran the numbers. We designed the work flow. We were convinced we could make a better product and match anybody's price. And when you throw in that we're part of FCI, we were sure we had the best package."

"What happened?"

"They went with an outside jobber. He's farther away. His price was a little lower, but not significantly. And he doesn't have the experience we have. So we're puzzled. No one ever gave us a straight story about why we didn't get the job. I looked into it, but there was an information blackout."

Carlos folded his hands and looked at them.

Nelson spoke for the first time. "We put a lot of effort into that proposal. And we'd be willing to do the same for your project. But are you serious about using North River, or are you just looking for a competitive bid?"

All eyes fixed on me again.

I didn't want to tell them at this point that they had the job for FlyingFox. There wasn't a job to have yet. Nor did I want to tell them I wouldn't manufacture elsewhere. I might. However, I needed a manufacturing team member now.

"As far as manufacturing the product goes, I can't promise you anything. But my preference is to work with you. I'm not talking with you just because I need a competitive bid, I can assure you of that."

Someone made a decisive first move toward the bun basket. This seemed to signal that the mood of the meeting had changed—the stickiest issue had been articulated, if not solved, and we now could proceed to the sticky buns.

"Maybe we should talk more about the project itself for a few minutes?" I suggested.

"Is it definitely going to be FlyingFox?" Nelson asked, a large coffee roll poised before his lips.

"It's not definite yet," I said. "What are your thoughts about it?"

"We've only been involved with early prototypes. But it's obviously a complicated product," said Nelson. "Very complicated."

"In what way?" I asked.

Helen spoke up. "It's got a lot of delicate little components," she said. "Plus, we've never worked with voice response before."

Nelson overlapped her. "And they're talking about using a housing material that's tricky to work with."

"Tell you the truth, Ron," Carlos said, "we haven't had a complete briefing from R&D. Nor have we talked to engineering. We don't know much about the product, so we're forced to speculate. We can't say at this time what FlyingFox is all about, or what it might require from us. We need to get more information."

Carlos had essentially shut them up, almost as if he didn't want them to get too involved yet without getting some indication of respect from R&D, engineering, or somebody.

"But I think I can speak for the group," he said graciously, "and say that we would be excited to work with you on the project."

Nelson and Helen exchanged glances. I couldn't read what they meant, but there was some reservation being expressed.

After another fifteen minutes of talk, Carlos walked downstairs with me and formally shook my hand.

"I'm sure we can solve whatever manufacturing challenges there may be." He looked me in the eye and gave me the most reassuring smile. "We'll be here for you."

I thanked him, but I left thinking: hidden agendas.

12. *Would She Rather Be Snorkeling?*

That afternoon, as soon as I returned from North River, I made the trek into the forbidding land of purchasing. I did so only to fulfill the promise I had made to Wesley and his engineers, secretly hoping I could convince Purchaser Phyllis Burch *not* to join the team.

I am a strong believer that each person has a great deal to offer an organization but will only contribute at the level required or demanded by that organization. However, as I pressed the button in the elevator (the elevator voice droning, "Doors closing—Building Three—Going up"), I realized that I did not include purchasing in this all-people-are-basically-good assessment. I saw them as drones. Process people. Paper pushers.

As the doors whished open, I further realized that this attitude was not a good basis on which to recruit a team member. I was operating with a prejudice, just as Martha had said I would.

Phyllis occupied one of what must have been a hundred nearly identical cubicles in the purchasing department, neatly lined along long, parallel corridors. The distinguishing decorative motif here was the inspirational wall poster. Beach scenes or the Matterhorn, small sailboats in the sunset or fields of soft-focus daisies, were superimposed with aphorisms about the meaning of life and work.

I found Phyllis in her cubicle, a woman in her mid-forties who seemed to fit my stereotype of the purchaser so accurately that I sensed it had to be a disguise. Small. Neat. Not a hair out of place. Half glasses. Lipstick in a slightly out-of-date shade. Surrounded by a stack of purchase orders. Staring into a page-length computer screen displaying columns of numbers. Husband, house, and children displayed in neat frames next to a pump dispenser of pink hand lotion.

There was a brightness in Phyllis' eyes, however, and an upward thrust of the chin that made me suspect she had not become an institutional, soulless pod person.

"Hello, Phyllis."

Phyllis had been recommended to me by the head of purchasing as a reliable, smart, and motivated worker, someone who might be willing to take on additional responsibilities.

"Hi," she said simply. "Will you have a cup of coffee?" She sounded as if providing me with a cup of coffee would give her immense pleasure.

"No thanks, Phyllis. I just wanted to spend a few minutes talking about a new assignment that I could use some help with."

"I'll be glad to help in any way I can." Was this the grace that results from a complete, unthinking acceptance of an un-changing, unchangeable, organizational status quo?

"I'm in the Technology Systems Group—"

"Yes, I know," said Phyllis.

"—and I'm leader of one of the New World teams."

"Oh yes, I know."

"Purchasing is an important part of the process, and I think it's an area that we often don't pay enough attention to, so . . ."

A cloud passed over Phyllis' face. She sighed almost imperceptibly.

"So you'd like us to expedite your purchase orders? I mean, we'll do the best we can, but, you know, there's only so much I can do. The procedure is very clearly defined, and if I have to get approvals from people who are traveling, then . . ."

As she talked, I tried to picture a typical day for Phyllis. Constantly beleaguered by dozens of supplicants, desperate for the speedy disposition of their scraps of paper, scraps that could bring life to whole projects or stall them indefinitely. That gave Phyllis enormous power, but a power that was entirely negative. Only by obstructing the flow of paper, and then miraculously restoring it, could Phyllis gain recognition. It was the power of the bottleneck. If she chose to use the power, she might be fawned over and flattered, but despised. If she chose not to use it, she would be ignored.

"Expediting is not really what we need help with," I said. "Although that will be greatly appreciated, of course."

Phyllis was stumped. "You want to reduce the supplier base? We're already working with Carlos out at North River to do that."

"No, that's not it at the moment. Although, again, that will be part of the effort."

"Oh." Phyllis seemed to be riffling through the litany of requests she had so often received. "Price. You want to try to work some volume deals? Across-the-board percentage discounts?"

"No, although of course we are after the best prices we can get."

Phyllis gave up. "That's our bag of tricks, Ron. I don't know how else I can help you."

She was perhaps suspecting that I had some more sinister motive in mind. Perhaps I was an agent of the Purge. Perhaps more layoffs were in store. Perhaps, once again, they would be made to pay thirty cents for coffee from the communal pot.

"Phyllis, I'm interested in how we could improve the purchasing process. Not just for my team, but in general." I could see in her eyes the reaction. Request for improvement is the same as saying I'm not doing a good enough job. She said nothing.

"I'm not talking about how you, Phyllis, do your job. I'm talking about how the system works."

Phyllis exhaled sharply, but still said nothing. She began to tidy up the stack of purchase orders beside her.

"I want you to be a member of our team. I want you to learn as much as you can about the project. To understand what we're trying to accomplish with the product, how it should look, how it should function. I want to share with you some of the financial information, so you can base your purchasing decisions on real knowledge. I want you to be alert to opportunities in the marketplace. If you can get a better price on something that meets our specs, get it. But if you feel that we need to spend more in order to meet our objectives, I want you to recommend that."

Phyllis' features had become fixed in place. I wasn't sure if she was listening. I felt like a warden who had just offered a lifer unexpected parole. She mistrusted the deal.

"No one has ever asked me to do that before," she said finally.

"No?"

"Never." She straightened in her chair. "Why me? Why are you asking me?"

"Your manager recommended you."

Another shock. "She did?"

"Yes. She said that you might be willing to take on some additional responsibilities and felt that you could easily handle them."

"You never know, do you. Wow." Phyllis shook her head. "You know, from the minute I started working here, I never could understand how we could buy things without really knowing what we were buying them for. And I thought, oh Phyllis it's just because you're stupid and you don't understand how this place works—because you don't have a business school degree. I was thinking about how I buy things at home. I mean, how can you go grocery shopping if you don't know who's coming for dinner?"

"Uh-huh." I had tapped into a rich vein of common sense that had never been mined before.

"But then, everybody else here just kept buying blind, and it seemed to work. So, after a while I stopped thinking about what the end product was, and concentrated on price and making sure all the PO's were filled out properly. I mean, it's not really my job to do any more than that."

"Now it is. I'm asking you to contribute more than that. What do you say?"

Phyllis shook her head. "I guess I don't know what you're asking me to do. But, if you want me, I'll do the best I can." She seemed proud to have been asked.

In that moment, I felt a great urge to help Phyllis succeed.

13. *The Glory That Is Kate.*

The rest of the afternoon was spent in my office, dealing with the 428 items that had accumulated during my two days away at the training course, and which demanded attention beyond my duties as New World team leader. I was just beginning to feel, if not caught up, at least slightly less swamped when I sensed a stir outside my office. A firm step on carpet. A burble of voices in its wake. An expensive, feral scent.

Kate pushed my already half-open door open wide. "Hi, Ronnie. Got a minute?"

The question was rhetorical. "Kate, for you?"

Kate, accompanied by her presence, now took command of my office and settled into a comfortable chair. She immediately kicked off her pumps and crossed ankles on my coffee table. "My feet are killing me," she said. She rubbed one instep and surveyed the place. "I don't see why you get a corner on the south side, Ronnie, when I have to suffer with a middle office facing west."

"Your office is bigger, Kate."

"I don't call four hundred square feet big."

"Huge is more like it." After three days of thinking about teams and leadership, I felt jarred by Kate's Old World concerns over status as measured by office size. "What can I do for you, Kate?" I asked.

"Fine, if you want to change the subject." She crossed her arms. "You can tell me how your team building is going."

"What do you want to know?"

"Who have you got so far?"

I could see no harm in telling her. I did.

"What about marketing communications?"

"No one yet."

"Good. I volunteer." She swung her legs off the coffee table and started looking for her discarded shoes.

In one way, I was eager to have Kate on the team. She had influence and tremendous energy. On the other hand, I didn't trust her motives.

"Why?" I asked.

Kate snorted. "Because you need me. You don't know distribution channels. You don't know advertising. You don't know PR. You don't know the sales force."

I didn't challenge this unfair assessment of my skills—I knew all of those things, although I was not a specialist in any. "But why do you want to take on the responsibility?" I asked. "I know you're extremely busy."

Kate slipped on her left shoe. "You think I can't handle the load? Ron, I'm not even close to full capacity."

"It's not that," I said. "But I'm asking for a major commitment to this team. I'm not interested in your playing an advisory role."

"Ron, you're so earnest. If I volunteer, I'll do what has to be done. You can trust me."

I was not convinced. "Are you joining any of the other New World teams?"

Kate registered shock. "How could I do that?" She slipped on the second shoe. "I may be asked to advise one or two of them. But that'll mean only an hour or two here or there."

If I knew Kate's style, it would be to volunteer for all the teams, choose the winner, and drop out of the rest when it suited her.

"Okay." If she was as clever as I thought she was, she knew perfectly well that I was skeptical of her commitment.

"Look, Ron," she said, shaking her right shoe at me. "I may not be the best detail person. But that's not what you need. You need the expertise I've got. You need big-picture thinking. I don't have to attend every housekeeping meeting and every team cookout to give you that."

Perhaps.

"By the way, Kate. Do you happen to know why FanFare is being manufactured by a jobber, instead of at North River?"

"Why, did you promise Carlos a favor?" she guessed.

"Maybe," I said.

"And what do I get if I tell you?"

I did not want to reduce team membership to a quid pro quo, at least not for a piece of information this trivial. "My undying appreciation," I said.

"Hmm," pondered Kate. She made up her mind that cooperation was the best course in this case.

"Because the FanFare people can't stand Carlos."

"Why not?"

"He gets peevish when he doesn't get his way."

"Peevish?"

"They've got nothing against the plant itself. They think it's first-rate. They just didn't want to deal with the Carlos temper tantrums."

She held up her hands: That's all she had to offer.

"Thanks."

She pointed at my heart. "You didn't hear it from me."

"Of course not."

"You owe me one."

14. *Private Pressures.*

Andrea and I had not had lunch together outside the building for months, but today it was clear Andrea needed to talk, and I realized that I needed to listen to what she had to say. We secured an outside table at the favored Fickie lunch spot, a local inn converted from a private mansion. We were shaded from the sun by an umbrella, but Andrea left her sunglasses on nevertheless.

"How did the move go?" I remembered that Andrea had taken a personal day to move into a new apartment.

"Fine."

"What's it like?"

"Expensive," she said. "It's more than I wanted to spend. But it's beautiful."

"Feeling a little stretched?"

"It's a big commitment having a three-year lease."

"You're not worried about job security, are you?"

Andrea sighed heavily. "No. No. Not really. It's just . . ." She broke off.

"Go ahead. Tell me what's on your mind."

Andrea exhaled. She removed her sunglasses. "Ron, I'm just worried about my whole career."

"In what way?"

"I thought I'd be further along by now."

"How do you mean?"

"My job really hasn't changed much in the two and a half years I've been here."

"You've taken on a lot more responsibility. You have your own projects. I feel like I never see you."

"I'm still a product marketing specialist. I should have more authority by now."

I hadn't been aware that Andrea had such a clearly defined timetable for her advancement. "Did I give you the impression that you would?"

"You said that a couple of years was the typical length of assignment for a specialist."

"That was true two and a half years ago. But don't forget the Purge. That slowed things down."

Andrea rolled her eyes. "I'm not forgetting it. That's what I'm worried about now. I really don't get what this New World thing is all about."

"You missed Ferry's talk about the vitals," I said. "Maybe I should run you through the thinking."

"No. It's mostly this team business. If I join the team, I just worry that I'll end up being everybody's assistant, and have even less authority than I have now."

"Why do you think that?"

"Because I don't know what my responsibilities would be. I get this sickening feeling that you expect me to be your side-kick."

"That's not what I expect."

"Well, what *do* you expect? What would my job be? How do you see my duties?"

"What would you like them to be?"

Andrea brightened. "I'm interested in the design aspects of the product. You know, the cosmetics and ergonomics. I also want some experience working with nonmarketing people. Manufacturing. Engineering. Field sales."

"Good."

"And I'd like to have some involvement in the conceptualization and implementation of the marketing and advertising launch."

"Kate has joined the team, you know. That's her responsibility."

"I can work with her. She'll need someone who can manage the day-to-day execution."

"Why don't you write up a job description as you see it, and we'll review it together." I suggested.

"Great. Give me a couple of days." She looked a little less anxious. Still, as we studied the menu, I could see that Andrea was not focusing on it. She let it drop.

"I hope you don't mind my obsessing about the team. But, if I were to lose my job—not because you fire me or anything, but because there's no role for me in this New World—I would be in trouble with the apartment."

"Aren't you sharing the costs with a roommate?"

Andrea bit her lip. "No, that's the other thing. You see, I thought I was going to be living with Mark."

"Yes?"

"But." She controlled her emotions with some effort. "It didn't work out."

New apartment. Loss of boyfriend. Fear of job change. A lot of stress.

"I'm sorry," I said.

"It's not your problem," she said. "I shouldn't have brought it up."

"I don't mind." I cared about her and wanted to help.

"I like working with you, Ron. I wouldn't have stayed at FCI if I didn't. And it's not that I don't want to help with the team," she said. "But I have to think about my career. I mean, you're all set. You'll come out of this thing fine whatever happens. But I think it might be disastrous for me."

"If it makes you feel any better, I don't feel all that secure about this either," I confessed.

She looked at me with surprise. "You don't?"

"No. I'm going into it with the assumption that it's a potentially career-limiting move." Career-limiting was Fickie talk for anything that might bring about corporate shame, exile, or outright termination.

"And you've got kids."

"Two lovely little brats."

"Is Janice working now?"

"Part time."

Andrea considered this.

"Why are you taking such a risk, then?"

I shrugged. "I had a vision."

"Of what?"

"Me on the cover of *Fortune*."

Andrea didn't know how to interpret this. However, hearing about my insecurity seemed to diminish her own. She giggled.

"Well, maybe you're right. What can I lose?"

15. *Fox Talk.*

I spent the afternoon staring into the windows of my PC.

To: Jasper
From: Ron
Re: New World Team project.

Here's the list of team members so far, with their responsibilities, in nonhierarchical alphabetical order by first name:

Andrea Carnovale, marketing/administration.
Carlos Garcia, manufacturing.
Jasper Lash, sponsor, guru, and source of all funds.
Kate Fiersen, marketing communications.
Martha Morgan, adviser.
Nick Yu, R&D.
Phyllis Burch, purchasing.
Ron Delaney, marketing, team servant, and coach.
Wesley Dunn, engineering.

After much team discussion, we have settled on FlyingFox as our product. We begin regular meetings next week.

To: Ron
From: Jasper
Re: Response to above.

Team members look good. Do you need somebody from finance? How about sales? I think FlyingFox is a good choice.

Keep me posted.

After I had finished exchanging E-mails with Jasper and several others, I came across the disk that Martha had given me. I slipped it into the floppy slot and waited while the computer churned. With a beep, the dreaded words appeared: ERROR READING DRIVE A. I did the natural thing and tried the same procedure over again in exactly the same manner, but banged the keys harder this time. I got the same message.

I ejected the disk. It looked okay. I was not eager to deal with technical problems of disks and formats, manuals and debuggers. I tucked the disk away to deal with later. I opened my teamwork file and, in a flash of creativity, renamed it Foxfile.

FOXFILE ENTRY:

• The experts call this the "forming" phase of a team's life. We've been successful in recruiting strong team members, but I have many questions about their commitment, motives, etc. Does Carlos have a hidden agenda for joining the team? Does Phyllis have the necessary competencies? Does Kate have a real commitment?

And I know that the team members have questions as well. I suspect the overriding one is—what is in it for them? What is the reward they get for taking this risk? Could this activity get them in trouble, and what kind of trouble?

At this stage, their questions can only be answered by talking about intentions and assurances. None of the traditional tangible types of rewards are being offered at the moment—money, promotion, perks, offices. Which means that people are joining the teams for other reasons. The joining instinct. Sense of duty. Inability to say no. Hope for personal gain. Coercion. Rational belief in teamwork. Fear.

At this moment, we are a collection of individuals. Now the job is to forge them into a group that thinks and acts for the good of the mission.

16. *Ritual Sniffing.*

We held the first formal team meeting the following Wednesday, a bright day in early May, in the Rugby Room. Everybody was there, with the exception of Carlos. I started at nine on the dot, without him.

"Good morning!" I greeted the team members. "Thank you for coming."

I scanned the faces around the table, trying to get a sense of their states of mind. Andrea, neutral. Wesley, fiddling with a mechanical pencil. Nick Yu, leaning eagerly forward, a stack of design drawings and papers at his side. Phyllis, nothing so much as a pencil on the table before her. Kate, Queen of marcomms, sitting at the far end of the table, expensive handbag at her side.

I referred to the agendas that I had distributed to each place.

"There are five items I'd like to cover this morning. First: introductions and everybody's role on the team. Second: team ground rules. Third: a quick review of the corporate mission and our team's objectives. Fourth: general discussion of the proposed project, FlyingFox. And fifth: next steps. And if there are any additional issues, we'll plan for open discussion at the end of the meeting. I'd like to wrap up by eleven. Now—"

The door opened and Carlos appeared.

"Sorry to be late, Ron," he said, slipping into the nearest available chair. "I had to stop by the plant this morning and I got tied up." Carlos was handsomely turned out in dark suit, brilliant white shirt, perfect dimple in the exact center of his tie knot.

Wesley took the opportunity of the interruption to change the subject. "Ron, could we talk about the time commitment for a minute?"

"Briefly." It was the last thing I wanted to talk about.

"How long do you think the weekly meetings will go on? And are you thinking they'll always be here in Building Three?"

"I expect the meetings to be weekly for the foreseeable future. No, they don't always have to be in Building Three."

Carlos joined in immediately. "Could I suggest that we do

a round-robin schedule? The manufacturing people have to add another forty-five minutes to the meeting time just for travel."

Nick Yu now nervously broke in. "And are you thinking this would be the regular meeting time? You see, we have an R&D staff meeting that usually meets Wednesday mornings, but we didn't have it this week because Dr. Z is out of town."

"Let's hold the discussion of time and place for the end of the meeting, please. I know it's an important issue. I know everybody's time is limited. But I want to focus this morning on the more substantive issues."

"Hear, hear!" said Kate, thumping the table with her fist. Whatever else Kate may be, she hates to waste time on petty details.

"Thank you, Kate," I said drily. "Now, let's take a few minutes and introduce ourselves to each other. Wes, would you start?"

Wesley returned the mechanical pencil to his shirt pocket. "Sure." He sat up. "I'm Wesley Dunn. Senior project engineer. I've been with FCI since the dawn of time. I was involved in the design and development of the original FanFare product. And right now I've got about twenty-eight engineers over in Building Four who are trying to deal with a computer system that's down."

"No wonder you're anxious about time, Wes," I said, practicing my active listening skills.

"I'm not anxious about time, I just don't have any to spare," he corrected.

"Wesley's job," I added, "is, of course, to coordinate the efforts of his team of engineers. But, more important, he'll be working closely with the R&D and manufacturing team members to make sure the product both realizes the original concept and is manufacturable."

"What, doesn't marcomms get any say in product development?" asked Kate.

"Of course you do," I said. "That's what the team is all about. Cross-functions, right? It's a collaboration."

"Good. Because this company usually forgets there are customers out there," said Kate. "And that's probably why we have fewer of them than we used to."

"I can assure you, Kate, that we want the customer and marketing perspective to influence product development."

"Good," said Kate. "It should."

Wesley looked down at the table. Nick Yu nodded earnestly. Carlos smiled ingenuously. The old animosity was already surfacing: technical versus marketing.

I kept moving. "Nick Yu is from research and development. FlyingFox is currently his project and he's going to be responsible for the key technologies and basic design concept."

Nick hugged the table and spoke rapidly. "Yes, I am Nick Yu. I've been with FCI a little over three years. My specialty is in software-based technologies. And . . ." He seemed to run out of gas. "I am very excited about bringing this product to market."

He stopped abruptly. Wesley, with a sly incline of his head, said, "How's the good Dr. Z, Nick?"

A nervous tremor from Nick.

I answered for him. "I'm going to be the liaison with Dr. Zanoski."

Wesley smiled. "Have you spoken with him yet?"

It was none of his business, but the smallest suggestion of conflict with Dr. Zanoski was sure to make the rest of the team nervous. "He's out of the country. But I'm on his calendar the day he gets back," I said. Wesley shrugged, and didn't push the issue further.

"Okay," I continued. "Andrea Carnovale will be focusing on design and marketing issues and will be responsible for general administration of the team. She'll be taking notes during this meeting. However, she is not—I repeat *not*—team secretary. But if you need support of some kind, Andrea probably can help you find it. Andrea?"

"My experience is primarily in product launch and brand support," she said. "But I'm interested in new-product development, and I want to learn more about the engineering and manufacturing side of it."

Andrea presented herself well. She came across as sincere and straightforward and I could see Wesley and Carlos respond to her interest in their jobs.

"To my left," I continued, "is Phyllis Burch. Phyllis is from purchasing and I've invited her to join the team, at Wesley's suggestion, because of the crucial role of materials and components both in product quality and in product cost. Phyllis."

"I guess after you've said I'm from purchasing there isn't much else to say, really," said Phyllis. "I handle the PO's and the RFQ's and I try to make sure what we order is what we get and that we get it at the best price."

Phyllis was nervous and deliberately underselling herself. I wanted her to say more.

"Phyllis has saved our butts on many occasions," added Wesley. "She's not saying it, but she's a lot more than a paper shuffler. She's an expert when it comes to dealing with suppliers."

Phyllis burst into a smile. "Oh, I don't know."

"I second that," I said, my annoyance with Wesley dissolving. I turned to Carlos. "Most of us know Carlos Garcia. He's head of the North River facility and our manufacturing guru."

"Thank you, Ron." Carlos drew himself up as if preparing to make a major speech. "As many of you know, I came to FCI about four years ago, with a mandate to turn the place around. I wanted to develop a Total Quality flexible manufacturing facility to rival any plant you might find anywhere in the world." He paused and smiled. "I am very proud to say that I have done just that."

Kate wagged her head. "All by yourself, Carlos?"

"We are *all* proud of our plant," said Carlos, glaring at Kate. "And we feel that not enough people within FCI know how good a facility it is."

This understandable viewpoint helped soften the impression of Carlos as a vainglorious self-promoter.

Finally, we came to Kate. "And Kate Fiersen. Many of you have worked with her in some capacity or other," I began. "Her job is to bring the marketing communications perspective to the development of FlyingFox. Particularly as it pertains to the launch, public relations, promotional programs, and advertising."

Kate arched her neck and touched her sleeve with a long forefinger. "Our focus is the customer. That's what we're all about." That seemed to be all she wanted to say. I decided not to add anything; Kate was more than capable of speaking for herself.

"I should add that although we all come from specific disciplines, I don't want us to think of ourselves as representatives of our departments. We're here to develop the best product we can and that means that everybody's view on everything is valid. If Nick has an opinion on advertising, we want to hear it. If Andrea has a reaction to an engineering issue, we want to hear that."

There were tentative nods.

"So," I said, "let's—"

"Ron?" interrupted Kate.

"Yes, Kate."

"Don't you think we ought to have a salesperson on the team? Someone who is out there in the field on a daily basis?"

I was not eager to add another person to the team at this stage, but she had a point.

"I agree," said Wes. "Those guys have the best insight into how customers are actually using our products."

"Okay," I said, making a note. "Let's see who we can find. If anyone has a suggestion, please let me know."

"And what about a finance person?" asked Phyllis. "Who's looking after the budget?" Phyllis was taking me at my word: Team members were encouraged to voice opinions on all topics.

"I'm responsible for the budget," I said. "And Jasper and the steering committee are the ultimate authorities when it comes to money. I think that may be enough representation from the bean-counting side."

A prejudicial epithet had emerged from the team leader's lips. I scurried to make amends.

"But you have a point, Phyllis. Let me take it up with Jasper. See if he really feels we need a financial voice at this stage." Of course, he had already suggested that we might include one, but I was resisting.

We moved on. Next subject: team ground rules. Simple but important stuff that clarified the basic expectations for every team member. Attendance at weekly meetings. Notification of me or Andrea if a team member couldn't attend. Communication of travel and vacation schedules. Handoff plan for when a team member was out of the office. Active participation at meetings. How to deal with problems or complaints. Distribution of a list of telephone, fax, mailstop, and E-mail numbers. Regular review and correction of team minutes.

Not much controversy there so we continued on to a review of the New World mission and the three "vitals," which by this time were well understood or at least much discussed, and then to the specific objectives of our team. Although the task and the deadline were daunting, they seemed to be clearly understood. We then came to the heart of the matter: FlyingFox. Nick began.

"Maybe I should say the reasons we are excited about FlyingFox. From the customer's point of view, we think it's going to be the most significant office machine to emerge in this decade. From the engineering point of view, it's challenging because we have to deal with multiple technologies in a single skin and provide some functionalities that have never been put into such a small, commercial package before. Plus, now with Product Delight, we have a new discipline, which is to consider the recycling, reuse issue."

Nick pulled a pencil sketch from his stack of drawings. He opened it and held it up for all to see—a complex bubble diagram.

"Let me take you through this conceptual drawing of the FlyingFox functionalities."

I looked around the room. I saw cartoon characters: mouths open, eyes glazed, bodies rigid. I hastily stepped in.

"Nick, perhaps before you go into detail, we could get some more general reactions to the product."

Nick stopped. "Oh," he murmured, weakly. "Sure. Okay."

He folds easily, I thought. Is that his normal behavior, or is it first-meeting nerves?

"Our reaction is that this is an extremely complicated product to build," began Carlos. "Not that we *can't* build it, of course. But there is one crucial issue in building this product that we don't yet have an answer to, and that is the housing material. It needs to have structural strength. It has to have good cosmetic properties. Heat resistance. And a lot of other properties. Plus, on top of everything else, it has to be a recyclable material. That's a tough combination."

Carlos paused to let this sink in.

Kate cleared her throat. "Who's going to design this thing?"

Nick raised his head. "Me." It came out small and unassertive.

"I'm talking about the human factors stuff. The feel. The color. The work of the switches," said Kate. "The Delight."

Wesley came to the defense of his fellow technical manager. "That's a collaborative effort between R&D and engineering. We have some people who are very good on the styling end of things."

"I'm not talking about styling," said Kate. "I'm talking about integrated design. Form and function as one. Products that look as good as they work. Products that scream at you 'Somebody with a brain and a heart and a soul put this thing together.' "

"We understand what you're talking about," said Wesley, on the defensive now. "That's what design engineering is all about."

"Oh, really?" retorted Kate, "I don't see it in most of the TSG products. I mean, FanFare is a good product, I'm not denying that, but I wouldn't call it delightful, would you?"

Cool silence.

"What I'm saying is that we better be damned sure we have the right people with the kind of creativity we need working on FlyingFox," Kate concluded.

The challenge seemed to cause Wesley to become more solidly a part of the group. "We will. You don't have to worry about that."

"Good," she said.

The discussion, if not harmonious, was lively. It was all healthy and useful, so long as no fistfights broke out.

"Could I just remind everyone that our task here is to produce the best product we can. It is not to defend our turf or win any interdepartmental battles," I said.

"Relax, Ron," said Kate mildly. "I just want to see that FlyingFox has outstanding design, so we can position it as an outstanding product."

The discussion continued for another twenty minutes, and then I outlined the next steps. Weekly staff meetings. Informal liaison with Jasper. The two formal presentations to the steering committee. The first presentation, to gain program approval, was our first clear milestone.

Finally, I invited open discussion.

"I have an issue," said Wesley. "The network. The computing environment. The only way all the people in this room can communicate right now is through E-mail. That's fine for memos and short messages. But we're all linked into different databases. And we don't have a good way to share files from different applications. For example, we have a link between engineering and R&D, but our communications with manufacturing are limited. We're still shipping paper drawings back and forth. If we're going to get this project done in a year, we need to speed things up."

I had not thought much about the implications of technology in helping or hindering our team functions.

Carlos waved his hand. "And we have no connection with R&D whatsoever. Nor do we have any integration with the sales and marketing database. We have our own manufacturing planning systems, but if we want to use sales and marketing data in our operations it has to be reentered. That's a pain and it wastes time and introduces errors."

"Do you think we should consult MIS?" I asked.

Carlos snorted and reared back, as if he had been slapped.

"I doubt it they'd be much help."

"Why not?"

"They're into protecting their mainframe. That's not what we need. We need a lot of power on the desktops, high-speed communications, and an open network that will encompass different operating systems and protocols."

"You're beyond me, Carlos," I said. "Can we identify this as an issue and discuss it more later?"

Carlos shrugged. "Okay. But it's not an easy one. It's going to cost money to get the capability we're after. And these machines don't get up and running just like that. It takes time. There's a learning curve." He crossed his arms and leaned back.

"The guy we need is Prandar," said Nick, out of the blue.

Wesley scoffed. "Sure, and maybe we can get Mahatma Gandhi, too."

"Who's Prandar?" I asked.

Nick looked at me in disbelief. "Prandar? You've never heard of Asvinkumar Prandar?"

"Ron, you ignoramus," said Kate.

"Just another of the thirty-seven thousand three hundred and eighty-two people I haven't yet met at FCI."

"Prandar is a software legend," explained Wesley. "He wrote the code for the original FCI B-series. He doesn't talk to mere mortals like us."

"He might," said Nick. "If the problem is impossible enough."

"Okay, I don't think we need Prandar yet. So are there any other issues?"

A brief pause, then Nick spoke up.

"Who will be reviewing our work? And how will our work on the team be evaluated? I mean, being on this team is not part of the objectives that were set for me for this year."

Andrea nodded vigorously. The younger members of the team, in particular, were concerned about their futures. Was this a sidetrack, a dead end, or a chance for quicker glory?

"You'll be evaluated by your current managers. However, the department heads have been directed by Ferry and the human resources people to include team participation as an evaluation criterion. Your manager is supposed to consult with me about your performance and include my comments in the overall evaluation."

Whether he liked it or not, this satisfied Nick. "Anything else?" I asked.

"Are we going to have a *place*?" asked Andrea. "A team office or room or maybe just a closet or something? Otherwise, we're going to be losing things. Or things will start piling up in my space. And as you know, there's no more space in my space."

"I hadn't thought of that," I began. At that moment the meeting-room door abruptly opened and two women walked in, in full conversation, as if they owned the place. When they saw us, they stopped. One of them looked at me.

"Are you signed up for this room?" she asked, annoyed.

"Yes," I said. "From nine to eleven-thirty."

The other woman looked skeptical. "We signed it up from eleven on." It was about a quarter past eleven.

"We're finished," I said.

As I ripped the scribblings from the flipchart, I thought: Perhaps Andrea is right. A cross-functional team with no physical space to call home is a truly amorphous entity.

17. *Fox Talk.*

To: Martha
From: Ron

First meeting of our New World team surfaced some of the animosities and prejudices that you talked about. Also, strong differences in personality type.

I think Wesley is sniping at me because he was my second choice. Any ideas about how to deal with him?

To: Ron
From: Martha

I would suggest talking with Wesley or sending him a note and telling him that you're glad he's on the team. Make him feel wanted.

To: Jasper
From: Ron

Highlights from our first New World team meeting:
  1. A dynamic group. Much participation.
  2. We are moving forward with FlyingFox.
  3. Do we need a finance member? Or can you and I handle that side of things? I'd prefer not to make the team any larger. We're already considering the inclusion of a field salesperson.
  4. Wesley brought up computing. Thinks we need more links between departments for sharing files/drawings, etc. Pondering a discussion with MIS. Any thoughts?
  5. Group feels that a dedicated physical space would be useful.

P.S. Attached please find minutes of first meeting.

To: Ron
From: Jasper

1. Great.
2. Fine. Let's talk about what the steering committee will expect as part of your program presentation. Let's also pick a date.
3. Why don't I get a financial person on board in an advisory capacity? You and I can review the financials with him/her. Yes, I think a salesperson on the team would be a worthwhile, even essential, addition.
4. Go ahead. Thorny issue, however, as it involves the whole organization. Cost is a major concern but, as I said, resources are available.
5. If you can find a space to claim, it's yours.
6. I hereby dub you Team FlyingFox.

P.S. Thanks for the meeting minutes. Keep them coming.

To: Andrea
From: Ron

1. Thanks for taking notes at the first meeting. I know you don't want that as a regular responsibility (even though you do it so well!). Any suggestions about how we can handle note taking from now on?
2. Would you be willing to take on the assignment of identifying a salesperson for team membership? Contact him/her, explain the team thing, and invite to our next meeting. We agreed that we'd look for ways for you to learn more about the other disciplines. Here's a chance.

To: Ron
From: Andrea

Yes. I'll try to find a salesperson. But don't you dare make me the corresponding secretary of this team. Why don't we hire a part-time secretary? Or better yet, rotate the job among all the members? I think it would be interesting to see how each person would record the conversations.

To: Wesley
From: Ron

Just a note to thank you for agreeing to join the New World team. And I especially appreciate your speaking up for Phyllis at the meeting. I have a feeling that your suggestion of including a purchasing person was a good one.

Thanks.

To: Ron
From: Wesley

If you think flattery and saying nice things will work with me, you're wrong. But I suggest you keep it up a little longer, just in case.

As I was reading, a ping alerted me to an urgent E-mail.

To: Ron Delaney
From: Dr. Emil Zanoski

I would appreciate meeting with you at the earliest possible convenience (today, if possible, please) to discuss FlyingFox project and Nick Yu's involvement.

18. *The Old World Asserts Itself.*

"Hello, Doctor."

"Ron, please sit down." Dr. Z, as he is referred to throughout FCI, is the antithesis of the absent-minded, chemical-stained research scientist stereotype. Tall, slim, elegantly dressed in conservative gray suits of European cut and brilliantly polished black cap-toe shoes, Zanoski is as smooth and controlled a manager as I ever have met. His corner office is all modern furniture and fixtures, cool glass and metal, pinpricked shades against the morning sun. He is an art lover, and large volumes of reproductions are stacked on his credenza. I feel that I am entering a private sanctum in a private home when I meet with Zanoski.

"How did your conference go?" I asked, by way of harmless, prebusiness banter.

"Very well." Zanoski was noncommittal, obviously uninterested in pursuing the subject. He had ascended to the role of FCI ambassador and senior scientist, and spent a large portion of his time on industry issues, meeting with members of government, the press, and our own senior executives. Yet he still kept a diligent eye on the functions of his own department, and managed to stay actively involved in a variety of projects in development. R&D was Zanoski's home and power base.

"I am concerned about the FlyingFox project," he declared.

"Why?"

"It is certainly a promising concept. In fact, I was involved in the earliest phases of its development."

"Yes, I know. It's an impressive product."

"But it simply is too far away from practical implementation. You will not be able to address all the technical issues satisfactorily within the eighteen months which I believe is your deadline."

"Twelve months."

"Let's not push the improbable into the absurd," said Zanoski, with a small, disdainful exhalation of breath. "And, although I think that Nick Yu will one day make a great contribution to FCI, he is still a junior member of this department and not ready for the demands of your project."

"I was hoping he'd get some help and support from others here in R&D."

Zanoski swiveled away from me in his black leather chair. "We have a completely full schedule," he said. "I'm sure you know that we are under tremendous time pressures already. And, like many other departments, we too suffered reduction in resources of money and manpower during the Purge. Nick is already working on several projects, and I don't see how he can take on more responsibility."

"But he has committed to do so. He's excited about FlyingFox and is currently working on a revised prototype. Besides, it was my understanding that you gave the go-ahead for FlyingFox to Jasper and the steering committee."

Zanoski swung back to me. "But I did not commit the resources of the department at the expense of our other projects."

"How do you expect FlyingFox to be developed? By an outside firm?"

"Implementation is not my responsibility." This was an excellent example of the kind of maneuvering that could kill the

New World teams. Senior managers professing support but delivering none.

"Do I take it that you don't really support the New World initiative?" I asked, wanting to pin him down.

"Of course I do. I think the mission is a worthy one. And I believe in closer working relationships across functions. But research is not like other functions in the company. What we are doing is creative. We are exploring the unknown. We cannot quantify our results as you can with service delivery or manufacturing. How do you measure the quality of an idea?"

"Can't you measure the number of R&D breakthroughs that are incorporated into new products? Can't you measure the time it takes to proceed from problem identification to problem solution?"

This irked Zanoski. Who was I to comment about his mysterious and jealously guarded process? "Sometimes you can. Sometimes you can't," he snapped. "A large portion of what we do here is basic research. We don't know what the application of the new knowledge we discover might be. Look at the laser. Look at fiber optics. Look at holograms. It can take decades for such new ideas to find practical applications."

"But FlyingFox doesn't depend on completely untested technologies."

"It incorporates advances in voice response that have never been achieved before. And it requires a sophistication of design of the user interface that Nick is clearly not experienced enough to achieve. And, finally, we have the recycling problem. I know that you have not identified a recyclable material for the housing yet. And I'm sure that the manufacturing people must be concerned about that."

"Carlos has discussed it with us."

Zanoski seemed to have finished the conversation to his satisfaction. "So, how will you proceed?"

I shrugged. "I'll take everything you've said into consideration. But my plan is to proceed as we are now. The structure of the New World teams is such that Nick has the freedom to join, if he feels he can handle the responsibility."

"Nick does not have the time—or the necessary competencies."

"But Bill Ferry has made it clear that commitment to teamwork is a condition of employment at FCI."

"The team I am concerned with is the one here in research and development. That is what I believe Mr. Ferry is referring to."

Zanoski was not to be convinced and I didn't want a man of his talent, power, and position against me.

"Doctor, has Nick been unable to fulfill his primary responsibilities so far?"

Zanoski faltered ever so slightly. "Not that I know of. But I have been out of the country for several days."

"If that's the case, aren't you're speculating?"

"I am merely trying to avoid a difficult situation."

I decided to try a compromise. "Why not allow Nick to work with the team on a trial basis, through our first program review," I said. "I'll speak with him and discuss your concerns with him. I hope that you will, too. Then, perhaps we both can keep an eye on his performance during the next few weeks. After the program review, we can talk again. Is that acceptable?"

Zanoski considered the idea. "All right," he said, "but if I see any indication that Nick's performance is jeopardizing our projects here, even before the review, I may have to take up the issue with Jasper."

"I would appreciate it if you'd start with me."

"Ron, I am afraid you are underestimating the seriousness of the issue. Your little team is a short-lived phenomenon. I am trying to maintain the reputation and improve the performance of one of the finest R&D operations in the industry."

He had an extraordinary ability to be condescending and gracious at once. "Doctor," I said, "you may be underestimating the seriousness of this team initiative. Bill Ferry, as I think you know, is supported not only by the steering committee, but by the board of directors."

Zanoski's eyelids drooped a fraction, as if this were all quite tedious. "So, Ron, you are convinced that Mr. Ferry can improve upon a method of product development that we have refined over a thirty-year period, and that has generated some of the best-known and most successful products on the market today?"

I decided on the short answer. "Yes."

Zanoski shook his head slightly. There was a double buzz on his phone. "I need to take this call," he said.

"Sure," I said. He nodded. I left.

I thought: I can give Nick Yu all the support in the world, but if Zanoski refuses to support him in his own department, he can't last.

19. *The Neighborhood Paradigm.*

Driving home, twilight, back-of-mind thinking:

At first, the idea of building a team sounds simple. Even fun. A nice "little" team, as Zanoski thinks of it. But the more you get into it, the more complicated and serious it becomes. It's as if the organization has a grain structure. As long as you follow the grain, you're fine. As soon as you cut across it, the going gets much tougher. But the very process of working against the existing structure has a liberating effect. Sparks fly, and sparks ignite new ideas.

The car in the lane behind me turned on its headlights. It became a dim bulky shape in the dusk, coming up too close behind me. Keep off my tail, please.

Let's see. How important was a physical center? A team room, as Andrea had suggested. An image of a clubhouse came to mind. The little rascals lolligagging around, dreaming up pranks. Probably a team room would be a nice-to-have, but not an essential.

What about skills? Zanoski certainly knows more about Nick's talent than I do. Maybe he doesn't have the experience or the sheer ability to turn FlyingFox into a viable product.

And how was the product going so far? It was in the hands of Nick and Wesley and Carlos and their people, until our internal review. I was letting them get on with their work, without sniffing around and trying to second guess them.

I pulled into the driveway and was gathering up my stuff when the lights in the neighbor's house came on. I realized that I had not seen any activity in the house for a while. Perhaps they'd been away? I didn't know. Maybe they were being held hostage? Possibly, although not likely.

Now a light came on in the house on the other side of ours. I saw a woman moving behind the window, someone I didn't recognize. Who was she?

I was struck by how it is possible to live in a neighborhood, in close proximity to a large number of people, and go about your daily business without being aware of their actions. I hadn't been inside half the houses that surrounded me. I had no conception of what many of the people in my neighborhood did for a living or how they occupied their days.

FCI had its similarities to a neighborhood. Separate dwellings. Separate lives. Loosely connected by a grid of formal streets and informal footpaths. But even small distances could make for complete separation.

As I toyed with the metaphor, I transported a neighborhood idea into the world of FlyingFox.

I decided it was time for a team barbecue.

20. *Sentimental Salesman.*

In the month we had left to develop our first presentation to the steering committee, Wesley and Nick and Carlos generated stacks of drawings and spent long hours tinkering with prototypes. I attacked schedules, budgets, and forecasts. Phyllis used her time to analyze and map the purchasing process, with an eye to streamlining it. Andrea tried, without much success, to get Kate to focus on marketing messages. In the give and take of routine team life, meetings and memos, ups and downs, we began to feel more comfortable with each other. The initial nervousness and surface anxiety slowly dissolved.

During that period, Andrea also worked with a vengeance to find the remaining team member, from sales, and she settled on a Fickie phoenix named Cub Wilson. A phoenix is an FCI employee who strays from the fold (takes a job at some unmentionable "other" company) and then returns and rises from his or her own ashes, bursting with new Fickie life.

Cub was traveling and couldn't join us until just a week before the presentation. His first free day coincided with our internal review meeting of all the elements of FlyingFox to date. He was to meet me in the lobby of Building Three so we could drive down together to North River, where the meeting was to be held. We had been rotating the meeting places, so no one was inconvenienced more than anyone else, and so that we'd all have a chance to have a look at the others' operations. This cross-cultural hosting had served to improve our understanding of each other's lives and operations.

Cub was not what I had expected. He was short and chubby. He did not wear the salesperson's requisite heavy ring, bracelet, and three-tone, four–time-zone watch. His suit was sand-colored, his tie a dull combination of pewter, olive, and gray. He carried an industrial green briefcase that looked bomb-proof.

"Hello, Cub," I greeted him.

"Yuh," said Cub, shaking my hand as if he had other, more important, things to do. "Let's take my car."

This distracted, fubsy little man led me out the revolving door, across the lawn, and to his car, still idling at the curb—a beautifully maintained, classic Mercedes coupe in tobacco color.

"A 1965 two-fifty SE," said Cub, anticipating my question. "Do you mind if I put the top down? I like the air. You don't smoke, do you?"

"No. Do you need help?" I volunteered.

"No. Works like a charm." He swiftly folded back the immaculate tan canvas, puffing lightly as he did so. "I smoke cigars," he said, slipping behind the elegant, ivory-colored steering wheel. "Hope you don't mind." Cub swung slowly away from the curb and began to talk. He did not light a cigar.

"I'm glad Andrea called me. She sounds on the ball. What's her background?"

"Marketing."

"I wasn't sure about joining at first, but she knew how to push my hot buttons. I like product development. And she started talking about how salespeople don't get involved in it enough, and how your group really wanted to get the customer point of view. We always make comments, you know, but it seems like they never get incorporated into the new products. I think we get asked for our opinions just to shut us up. Just so management can say we asked you. But it sounded to me like Andrea was serious."

Cub slowed at the stop sign, then eased out onto North River Road.

"I'm glad she gave you that impression. We are serious."

"What bothers me the most is that I don't think enough Americans care about products. You know what I mean? The Europeans love their products. The Japanese love their products. But we don't. Most of us just love money. But I like the way good products work. And I think customers do, if you give them something that really does work."

Cub shifted down. The car soared along the country road.

"That's what Product Delight is all about."

Cub ignored me. "I saw a show about a toy company in Germany," he said. "They spent ten years perfecting their little plastic figures. Adults might think they're dull. But kids love them."

I thought of Emma, who owned a huge tub of figures and animals and conveyances and could create and recreate scenes endlessly with them. "Yes."

"I tell you, Ron, the show made me cry," said Cub, looking a little teary-eyed as he said it. "It was the old story. The marketing people kept telling the designer that he should put in electronics and moving parts and motors and stuff. The designer said no. His customers didn't want them. And he was right. He was stubborn. He was right. And it worked."

"What's your impression of FlyingFox?" I asked.

"I don't know yet. I've got an open mind. But I will have to say what I think."

"That's why we want you on the team. We want your opinions and your ideas.

"Okay." Cub flipped on the radio, and we heard the final strains of the national anthem, followed by a cheer, and then the gravelly voice of a baseball announcer starting the play-by-play.

"I love baseball," said Cub. "I'm a big fan. Do you mind if we listen for a minute?"

"Sure." I chuckled. "Are you a Cubs fan? Is that where you got your name?"

"What?" Cub seemed confused. "Oh, no," he said, finally realizing the connection I was making. "No. My mother thought I looked like a bear when I was a kid."

21. *Cub Leads the Cheer.*

I introduced Cub, the new member, to Kate, Carlos, Wes, Nick, Phyllis, and Andrea. He shook hands all around, beaming when he got to Andrea.

"You're Andrea! You ought to be in sales!"

Andrea smiled.

"No, really!" insisted Cub. "When you first suggested I join this team, my reaction was, forget it, who needs it? But you convinced me it was for my own benefit. That's good sales stuff. Really, Ron, you might consider getting her out into the field for a couple of years."

"Not a bad idea," I said. "That way she won't take my job."

"Don't be ridiculous," said Andrea, embarrassed at all the attention.

"Okay, let's get started," I said. Cub stationed himself in the last row and nestled down into the plush blue seat, as if waiting for a movie to begin.

"I can't overemphasize how critical this presentation is," I began. "It's our first chance to present ourselves as a unified group—"

Good-natured sniggers from Wesley and Nick.

"Okay, reasonably unified group, and our first chance for feedback from the steering committee. Not to mention the fact that we can be cancelled. So, not to make anybody nervous, but this is life or death."

No further sniggers.

"We have two hours for the presentation to the steering committee, as you know. I'd like to see us finish the formal part in an hour and half. Half hour for questions." We had a brief discussion of how to proceed with the rehearsal and decided to run through the entire pitch and then make comments.

I was first up, and started by painting a picture of how our target customer of some two years hence would be using FlyingFox. "Picture, if you will," I began, "a machine about the size of today's personal laser printer. It is not the dull cream color of most office machines today, but rather a muted green."

I heard what I took to be a snort from the back of the room, in Cub's direction. "Green?"

"Now, the user approaches the machine and speaks to it. 'Start, please.' A gentle hum is heard. The machine responds, 'Ready.' "

There was another rustle and vocal rumble from the rear of the auditorium. "It's gonna talk?"

"Cub," I called out to the back of the room. "I wonder if you could hold your comments until we finish."

"Yuh," agreed Cub, pleasantly. "But are you serious about this stuff?"

"Yes, we are."

Cub confined himself to just a few under-the-breath comments as I continued, and I then handed the floor over to Nick Yu. He had received some coaching, and his comments were brief and to the point. He left the impression, however, that there were a number of technical issues that had yet to be addressed.

Wesley followed Nick, and it was clear that he had not prepared his remarks. He rambled and got sidetracked, cracked inappropriate jokes, and seemed to believe that his expertise would be taken for granted.

Carlos then outlined the manufacturing plan, including a brief discussion of the candidates for the material, which had not been determined yet. Kate talked in a disconnected way about her approach to marketing and promoting products in general, without saying a word about FlyingFox in particular. I concluded with a budget and schedule review.

When we were done, we gathered into a circle to discuss the presentation. Cub wandered to within two or three rows of where we all sprawled around the small stage, some sitting on the floor, some in chairs.

"Okay, let's review the presentations," I said. "All comments are welcome, including comments on presentation style. But please, no unfair personal attacks. No turf tirades. We want to make this the best presentation we can. Let's start with me."

And so began three intense hours of review and discussion, which provided a good workout for my meeting skills-- keeping the discussion on track, eliciting response, fielding ideas ranging from the reactionary to the irrelevant, active listening, summarizing key points.

We argued the merits of my opening vision. We talked

about the problem of the housing material. We figured and re-figured budget numbers and forecasts. We wondered about promotional approaches. Above all, we tried to assess whether the presentation would convince the steering committee that FlyingFox was a viable product.

The most telling moment came when I asked for comments about Wesley's presentation. The room fell silent.

"I know. Perfection," said Wesley, facetiously. No one laughed.

"I think it was too long, Wes," said Carlos finally. "I think you need to tighten it up."

Wesley was surprised and offended. "There's a lot that we need to cover," he said. "I'm not going to get up there and give a fluffy presentation that glosses over the issues."

"I don't think anyone is suggesting that, Wes," I said. "But we are running long and we need to keep it clean and focused. How would you summarize the key points you want to make?"

Wes ignored me. "Look, I never do that well in these rehearsals. But when I get in there, I'll be fine. Most of those people know me anyway."

"But we want to sound like a unified group, Wesley. A team," I said. "That's what they're looking for, as well as our product ideas. They want to get a sense that we're working together and can solve whatever problems we're going to face."

"We're not going to solve the problems in a group, anyway," said Wesley. "When it comes to engineering problems, the only way they get solved is by an engineer sitting down alone at the computer or at a drafting table. That's how it happens."

"Wesley, I know how you feel," spoke up Nick. "But I think you're getting too technical in your descriptions."

"They just want to know that you think we can do this," said Kate, cutting through it all. "They want to know that Mr. Experience is on board."

Wes fell silent. It was Carlos who finally asked the pivotal question.

"*Are* you on board, Wes? Do you think we can convince the committee to support FlyingFox? Do you think it's a good product, after three weeks of working with it?"

Everyone looked at Wesley. Before he could answer, however, Cub spoke up.

"You know what I think?"

He got up and moved into the front row. His eyes were gleaming. He spoke in an awed whisper.

"I think it is Fan-FlyingFox-tastic!"

He clapped his hands and leaped up. "What a product! What a thing to sell! People are going to go nuts! They're going to love using it! It's going to make their lives wonderful! What the hell are you people quibbling about? We're going to sell a zillion of these things. It's great!"

And then he sat down again and crossed his chubby legs. There was a moment of silence, and then we all started to laugh.

"Yeah, okay, okay," Wesley said, when everything had quieted down. "I'm on board."

There was a cheer.

"But look," Wes continued, "I don't care how much of a team member I am. I still believe the real creative work gets done individually. You'll never convince me otherwise. Never."

"Hey, you don't have to love us, Wes," said Kate. "You just have to work with us. There's a difference."

After the meeting, Cub left to visit a customer so I planned to drive back to the office with Andrea. She went to retrieve the car and I stayed with the video equipment. Kate, who had lingered behind, took the opportunity to pounce on me.

"You blew it with Wesley, Ron."

"What do you mean?" I was not expecting this.

"The guy is a hopeless presenter. If he gets up in front of the steering committee and rambles like that they're going to tell us to go home. I don't want to be associated with any presentation like that. You've got to do something about him."

"What do you recommend?"

"Get him some speaker training. Kick him out. Let Nick do the pitch. Anything. I can't believe you were so gentle on him in there. Everybody knew he was rotten, but nobody told him."

"I think we told him."

"You were mighty subtle about it. Wesley needs a much bigger whack on the side of the head. You can take this coach approach a little too far. Now and again you're going to have to kick people in the butt."

"Why don't *you* work with him?" I suggested. "You're a good presenter. You could probably whip him into shape in a couple of hours."

"I will. You make the suggestion to him, and I'll do it. It would give me great pleasure to tighten him up."

"I probably won't phrase it that way to him."

"Say it any way you want, Ron. It amounts to the same thing."

Kate's attack had put a dent in my confidence. Both Andrea and I were uncharacteristically quiet on the drive back to Building Three.

"How do you think that went?" I asked finally.

"I think we'll be all right. If Wes doesn't ramble too much."

"Kate just blasted me for that. She volunteered to help him with his presentation. More or less."

"That would be fun to watch."

"Thank God for Cub, though," I said. "He galvanized everybody. That kind of enthusiasm is infectious."

"Do you think so?" she asked. "You don't think people react to that as just glib sales talk?"

"No, I think Cub says what he thinks, and people respond."

"So you think he was a good choice?" Andrea shot a sideways glance at me. I realized I had almost missed an opportunity to provide her with some recognition and praise.

"Early indications are that he was an excellent choice. And I want to thank you for all the legwork you've done."

"I'm not fishing for praise."

"I'm not making it up. I'm not sure I would have had the guts or the judgment to recommend Cub."

"I had a feeling about him. Plus, I really checked out his credentials with several Fickies, and I even talked with a couple of customers about him. They love the guy."

I looked at Andrea afresh. She had an astute sense of what people could offer and how they would fit in a group. A necessary managerial skill, I thought.

"You'll probably have my job one day."

"I was thinking more along the lines of being your boss."

"There are no bosses in the New World," I said.

"We just don't call them that," she said.

"Is that what you think? You think this is all a sham?"

Andrea considered for a moment. "No. I think this team has a chance of being successful. I just don't think a big company like ours changes that fast. The New World could evaporate overnight, and we'd find ourselves back in the Old World again."

"But you have more optimism now that it's going to work than you did at the beginning. Why?"

"I hate to say it, but I think you're doing a pretty decent job so far. You listened to my worrying. We worked out my job responsibilities. Nobody has called me a secretary yet. And I've done a couple of interesting things, like recruiting Cub, that I wouldn't have done otherwise."

"I'm relieved."

"You are. Why?"

"The team needs you."

Andrea beamed for a moment, and then the smile abruptly faded and she turned to me. "Do you think Kate's doing a good job?"

"Kate is unpredictable, and her contribution to date has been minimal."

Andrea looked at me in earnest. "If she drops out, I can take over. I have a lot of ideas about marketing FlyingFox and how to deal with the launch. If it comes to that, will you consider me?"

"Of course I will." I wished that Kate would disappear at that moment so I could give Andrea her chance.

22. Reality Checks and Rumors.

We spent the following week refining our presentation and working to shore up the weak spots in the FlyingFox program. My own feeling was that although the functions and basic workings of the product were coming along, we were a long way from Product Delight. And we still were nowhere on the housing material.

I offered Kate to Wesley as a speaker coach and, surprisingly, he accepted. They were closeted together for almost three hours one day and emerged with no evidence of bloodshed.

During that week, I also did an informal poll of the other New World team leaders, trying to get a sense of how their efforts were progressing. I learned that in comparison to our (friendly) rivals, we were in decent shape. The C&P team was full of confidence. But the corporate team, code-named Ficus, was limping.

"You know, I was skeptical of this team approach from the beginning," Dick Eggart, the Ficus team leader, confided. "And nothing has changed my mind."

"What do you mean?"

"I can't get people to commit to the team. Everybody's too busy with other projects and I can't force them to care about Ficus. Have you had that problem?"

"Commitment is a problem," I agreed. "But our core group is pretty solid now."

"You're lucky. I've had four team members drop out already."

"How many people do you have on the team?"

"We started with eighteen."

"That sounds like a lot, Dick. The consultants said to keep the core group small. Ours is about six."

"But now I'm glad I had so many to start. If the attrition rate keeps going like this, we'll be down to six or seven people before long."

"Perhaps people are dropping out precisely because your group is too large."

"Maybe. But no one has told me that's the reason." There was a pause at the other end of the line. "I find it ironic, really," he mused. "Everybody talks about empowerment and pushing authority down into the ranks. But now we've got these teams, which are supposedly all about empowerment, and they're not working. People need an authority figure to tell them what to do."

"Do you think your team members are clear on what they're being asked to accomplish?"

"Ron, please. I went to the training course too, remember.

I know the jargon. 'Senior management commitment. Define objectives. Establish responsibilities.' But how can I be clear on what my team members are supposed to do when I'm not comfortable with what *I'm* supposed to be doing?"

"What do you mean?"

"I feel like I'm supposed to be telling everybody what a great job they're doing, even when they're doing a rotten job. You know, constant recognition and reward. But I can't do that. It's phony. I expect superior work from everybody, and I don't think it's my responsibility to teach them their jobs. They're all professionals. Why should they care about a pat on the back from me?"

"Isn't it the team leader's function to help them do their best work?"

"How the hell can I do that? I don't know anything about design. I don't know anything about advertising. The team members are supposed to be the experts in their departments. And I'm supposed to be the expert in managing it all. It's a simple, tried-and-true division of labor."

"But don't you think it's a matter of trying to understand their concerns? Just getting them together and working out the issues?"

"We've been doing that for weeks now. We keep going around and around in circles. R&D has an idea. Manufacturing says we can't build it. Engineering wants to do it one way. The marketing people say it's ugly. Our staff meetings are worse than therapy sessions."

"How about the product itself? Are you making progress with it?"

"That's what I'm saying. We haven't even settled on a product yet!"

"But the presentations to the steering committee are next week."

"We're going to present two or three options. Get some feedback from the steering committee."

"But isn't that just forcing the decision back onto them?"

"I don't see it that way. It's their job to steer us, after all. We could go in any one of a dozen different directions, but we want to make sure the one we choose has a blessing from the powers that be. We could expend a lot of effort developing some harebrained product and they wouldn't approve it and then we'd be two months behind. This way we're covered."

"But isn't that Old World thinking? Ferry is telling us to go for results, to take some risks. And you're saying you've got to cover your ass."

Dick's tone lowered, as if he were talking to a misguided child. "Ron, you're right. Ferry says he wants us to take risks. *Us.* Not him. He sits on his throne, we come forward and kneel before him bearing our team projects. He anoints the ones he likes and the ones he doesn't like are thrown to the wolves. That's the risk he wants us to take—the risk of pissing him off."

"I don't agree. Everything he has said so far, and everything Jasper has said, makes me believe this is a genuine initiative."

"I'm not the only one who feels this way." Dick's tone dropped even lower. "Take the marketing gal I had on the team. She was one of the first to drop out. She told me she thinks the whole New World business is simply the prelude to a major housecleaning."

"Who's that?"

"Kate Fiersen."

"She was on your team?"

"For about an hour and a half. Fortunately, I had two other marketing types to fill in."

So Kate *was* sampling other teams. Obviously, her judgment about Ficus had been correct. Although I found her behavior devious, I also felt an absurd pride that she was still attending FlyingFox meetings.

"One of the other marcomms types had a good idea. We made up some Ficus team T-shirts. Corny maybe, but the demand for them was unbelievable."

There was a blip on the line.

"Dick, I've got another call coming in. Good luck to Ficus."

Dick did not want to hang up. "I'd love to talk about this some more. Why don't we have lunch, or maybe dinner, sometime this week?"

Team leaders are supposed to help each other, but I had no interest in devoting any more time to Dick or to Ficus. "Listen, I'm completely booked until after the presentation. Why don't we plan to get together after that?"

"Good," said the Ficus chief. "I'll call you."

I punched into the incoming call, doubting that there would be a Team Ficus after the program reviews. It was Cub calling from his car.

"I'm picking up some worrisome rumors, Ronnie."

"What are they?"

"MarTech is working on something that sounds pretty much like FlyingFox."

"How do you know this?"

"I had lunch with a guy who sells specialty plastics to a supplier that he knows sells to MarTech. Now, my guy was calling on the supplier one day and the buyer there said that one of the supplier's clients—which my friend assumed to be MarTech—was looking for a specialty material for some new product. The buyer gave my pal the specs on the product, and he showed them to me. It doesn't take a genius—although fortunately you do have one, I'm talking about me, Ronnie, don't forget that when it comes to bonus time—it doesn't take a genius to figure out that this MarTech product is pretty similar to what we're working on."

"Any idea how far along they are?"

"If they're talking to suppliers, they have to at least be into the prototype stage. Maybe getting ready for pilot production."

"How sure are you it's MarTech?"

"Eighty-five percent. But we could be wrong."

"Can you show me the specs?"

"He wouldn't let me take a copy. It's not illegal or anything, but his customer wouldn't be too thrilled if MarTech discovered the specs had gotten into my hands."

"What do you suggest we do about this?"

"Keep working and keep our ears open."

Cub's news was distressing. Not only was it worrisome in relation to FlyingFox and its potential in the marketplace, it put me in a ticklish spot. Should I tell Jasper? Or the steering committee? Would they be more or less likely to fund the project if they foresaw tough competition in the marketplace?

FOXFILE ENTRY:

- Competitive maneuvers and marketplace conditions used to seem remote to the middle layers of managers at FCI. We didn't feel responsible for them, or capable of influencing them.

Now that I have direct responsibility for a new product, I am much more sensitive to what's going on in the marketplace. This is what "ownership" is all about. When you feel directly responsible for the fate of a product, you feel the connection between yourself and the customer/marketplace much more directly.

It is a much more effective method of getting people "close to the customer" than telling them they should be.

23. *I Do a Little Light Reading.*

The Thursday evening before our presentation to the steering committee I spent reading. In the past few weeks, I had dipped in and out of *My Years with General Motors,* Alfred Sloan's book, which provided me with a useful perspective on how the prevailing organizational structures (at FCI and elsewhere) had developed.

Tonight, the pile of books at my elbow included *20/20 Vision* by Stan Davis and Bill Davidson, *In the Age of the Smart Machine* by Shoshana Zuboff, *The Change Masters* by Rosabeth Moss Kanter, *The Fifth Discipline* by Peter Senge, and *Survival of the Fittest* by Philip Himmelfarb.

What struck me was how much agreement there was among the authors and experts that the corporation (as an entity) is undergoing fundamental change. As a result of the maturation of many industries, global competition, and the proliferation of information technology (and several other factors), organizations are struggling to redesign and reengineer their processes and their structures, moving away from the hierarchical and rigid to the diversified, empowered, and flexible. This is obvious to anyone who is alive and alert and trying to function in a big company today.

What I found so compelling about the reading, however, was that most of the observers and consultants considered the role of the team—teams like FlyingFox—crucial to the survival and success of organizations today. It made me feel that Team FlyingFox was not an isolated, risky experiment. We were playing an important role, involved in the difficult, hands-on work of developing ways for a diverse, geographically separated group of people to perform successfully together.

I heard the back door close and, in a moment, Janice banging around in the kitchen. She appeared with a beer in hand and folded herself into the couch. She looked tired.

"What are you reading?"

I showed her the book and she grimaced. "Got a lot of good jokes, I bet."

"How was the meeting?" I asked.

"Oh, we're about to start a major fund-raising drive, and we can't even articulate what the purpose of our organization is."

"That's the hardest part. That's why you need a Ferry and a Jasper and a steering committee."

"Are you actually praising your managers, Ron? I haven't heard talk like that in a while." She sipped her beer.

"I was thinking of projects I've been on in the past when *we* couldn't articulate our purpose. I know how frustrating it is. But that's not the case with FlyingFox, and I guess I have to give Ferry some credit."

"It's certainly better than spending half your meeting time trying to figure out what you're doing rather than actually doing it."

"Perhaps you'd like me to come to your next meeting and straighten things out."

Janice ignored my kind offer and changed the subject. "How many people are we expecting at the party?"

We had settled on a Saturday late-afternoon-into-evening team barbecue, and Janice had volunteered to buy the supplies.

"Everybody's coming. Except I'm not sure about Jasper."

"Okay. And how did everything go with FlyingFish today?" She picked up the television guide, a signal that she was not interested in hearing the long answer to that question tonight.

"FlyingFox," I corrected her.

"So long as it flies." She yawned. "Is there anything worth watching on TV?"

24. *The Verdict.*

The presentation went over well. I felt confident, and the team members were convincing and enthusiastic. Nick controlled his propellor-head tendencies. Wes, thanks to Kate, rambled very little. Carlos did not linger too long on the wonders of North River. Phyllis talked about ways to streamline and reduce the cost of the purchasing process. Kate, at the last minute, had called from the airport—an emergency trip out of town. Andrea made the presentation in her stead.

We finished in just over two hours. As we were leaving the boardroom, we met Dick and the Ficus team on the way in.

Dick grabbed my elbow. "What kind of mood are they in?"

"They seem receptive."

"I took your advice," continued Dick. "We're presenting just one product, not two."

"So you reached concensus."

"I made an executive decision."

"You mean you made the choice without agreement from the team?"

"I had to. The ones who don't like it can either live with it or bail out."

"That may come back to haunt you."

I heard coming-to-order sounds inside. "I better get in there," said Dick, scurrying away.

"Good luck," I said, knowing that luck had little to do with it.

That afternoon, around two-thirty, I got the call from Jasper. "Come on up," he said, with a friendly, tired tone that could indicate either success or commiseration.

I was puffing slightly when I reached his office, having run up the back stairs three at a time. I paused before knocking, trying to regain the calm and composure one expects of an experienced, senior manager of one of America's most venerable and well-known companies.

Jasper opened the door before I could knock. He was in his shirt sleeves, and the white shirt fabric was so new and lustrous that it rustled as he fiddled with the ever-present Mont Blanc.

Still looking at the pen he said, casually, "You can stop panting. You've got the go-ahead."

I let out a whoop.

"Don't go manic. Come in, we have a lot to talk about."

I followed Jasper in. He leaned against his desk, as usual, and continued playing with the pen.

"What were the reactions of the committee?"

"FlyingFox is the riskiest of the New World team projects. As we see it, you have at least three challenges to overcome. One is design. This is a product that will sink or swim on brilliant design. Two, which links in with number one, is the housing material. You obviously don't have a solution yet, but you'd better by the next presentation. Three: positioning. FlyingFox is going to need special handling when it gets to the launch. If you don't position and present it properly, it won't get into the hands of the right customers or get the support of the sales force. It might just wither on the vine."

"Fair enough." Jasper had a keen ability to boil the issues down to a few key, well-articulated thoughts. "Although you might have gotten a stronger impression of the marketing plans if Kate had been in the meeting."

"I doubt if she would have done much better than Andrea. Anyway, we have two strongly felt suggestions, but, in the spirit of the New World, I wouldn't go so far as to call them directives."

"What are they?"

Jasper finally put his pen down, and channeled his excess nervous energy into attending to his All Things Bald collection. He picked up the phrenology skull and stroked its smooth wooden top.

"First, we have concerns about Nick Yu's role in this project."

I started to speak in Nick's defense, but Jasper raised his hand.

"It's not his abilities or commitment we question. It's his ability to negotiate the gantlet that Dr. Z will construct for him. That's a reality, and one you'll have to deal with. If I need to talk with Emil, I will, but I don't want it to come to that. And, two, which is perhaps more important, is that nothing in Nick's track record suggests he can create the kind of exterior design that we think Fox is going to need."

"You're suggesting we get another person on the team?"

"I'm suggesting that you consider working with an outside firm as a design development partner, one with experience in designing and positioning new products."

My first reaction was defensiveness for Nick. Even now, they don't trust us. Jasper anticipated, or perhaps read, my reaction. "Ron, don't take this as an insult to the composition of your team. You've done a superb job assembling a broad-based, diverse, highly capable group of people. But few teams have all the competencies they need. You could recruit another person perhaps, but I think it makes more sense to partner with an outside firm in this case."

I said nothing.

"Just consider it," said Jasper. "It might be exciting for you."

He put the phrenology skull back on the coffee table and now picked up two black billiard balls, both eights. He tried to roll them around in his hand.

"Budget. We're prepared to commit to roughly the budget you and I put together. But the committee thinks it would be better if you or one of your team members worked directly with the financial adviser."

"I'll do that."

"That's it, then," concluded Jasper. "Oh, except the steering committee wants to have regular reports from you. Say, every month. Not necessarily a formal presentation on the order of the one you gave yesterday. Just progress reports." He tried to swirl the billiard balls again and dropped one on his foot.

"Damn!" He jumped up and down in pain, cradling his foot and polished kiltie loafer in both hands. "Is there anything else we can do for you, Ron?" he asked, still jumping.

"You can come to the barbecue."

"I'll try," moaned Jasper. "If *Rigoletto* gets out at a reasonable hour."

FOXFILE ENTRY:

• The relation between the team and its sponsor can be an edgy one. We want Jasper to keep his distance and give us our "empowerment." We also want to know he's there to support us if necessary—for

example, if the conflict with Zanoski gets too difficult. And yet, as team loyalty grows, we can find ourselves closing ranks even against our sponsor—witness my reactions to Jasper's comments about Nick.
We have to get the balance right.

25. *Around the Campfire.*

Saturday was a soaring June day, brilliant and invigorating. In the morning, with the promise of a movie the next day, I coaxed some help out of both kids. Kip volunteered to hang lanterns above the barbecue. Emma, who has an artistic bent, leaped at the assignment of creating a sign for the driveway. She decided to draw a flying fox.

"Is there really such a thing?" she asked.

We consulted *Webster's Third New International* together.

"FLYING FOX. Definition number one. A fruit bat."

"Yuck," said Emma.

"And definition number two. A carrier (as for mining material or produce) operating on cables over a gorge or other obstacle."

I responded to that second meaning. Our FlyingFox team was a way to get over the gorge that separated the Old World and the New.

"I'd rather think of it as a fox that can fly," said Emma. "A fierce business fox with wings."

Emma spent the next half hour creating a reddish-purple, long-furred creature, sharp of jaw and eye, soaring through a brilliant sky. Everybody liked it so much, it was adopted as our team logo.

Two minutes after five. FlyingFox sign in place. Lanterns successfully hung. Food ready for barbecuing. The bright, surging chord of a klaxon horn signaled the arrival of Cub, claiming the dubious honor as first guest. I strode across the lawn to greet him, and was nearly blinded by his attire as he wriggled from the Mercedes. Striped shorts in an array of sherbet colors, raspberry polo shirt, and three-toned boat shoes with fluorescent pink laces. Porkpie hat and wraparound biking sunglasses with metallicized lenses.

"Hey, Ronnie!" he called merrily. "Yes, thanks, I would like a drink."

I fixed Cub a vodka and grapefruit juice, and we talked about his career with FCI.

"I was a Fickie for twelve years, from 1973 to 1985," said Cub. "Then I went out on my own. I repped for a bunch of companies, and I made a lot of money but I got lonely. Then I worked for a little startup company, and they were so confused they couldn't figure out which way to put their product in the packing case. So, last year I said, the hell with it, I'm going back in."

He took a sip from his drink. "To FCI, I mean. But I was in the retail group in my first life. This is my first tour with your group."

"How's it going?"

"Things are softer out there than you think."

"What do you mean?"

"FanFare Two is late, and the market is just about saturated for a FanFare One kind of product. Customers are just buying FCI on price deals, volume discounts, cheap service contract promotions, and the strength of long-term relationships. But if a competitor came along with a machine that offered even a few more features than FanFare, I think customers would run to buy it."

"Any more news about that MarTech product?"

"I did pick up another rumor." Cub looked uncomfortable. "That FCI is coming out with a new product, code named FlyingFox."

"Who did you hear this from?"

Cub swirled his ice cubes. "I was at lunch with a customer. She said, 'I hear FCI is bringing out a new product' and then described all the things that she heard it was going to do that in fact FlyingFox will be able to do."

"How did she hear about it?"

"She wouldn't tell me. But she asked if we knew about the MarTech product."

"What did you say?"

"I said, 'How'd you like to be a beta site for FlyingFox?'"

"So, you essentially confirmed that we have this product."

"No, I told her she could be a beta site, that she'd get a

couple of FlyingFox units free, but that she couldn't talk about it until we delivered them."

"I'm not sure that was the best way to handle it, Cub. I'd appreciate it if you called me before you make any deals like that again."

"Ron, we were in the restaurant. Who knows who she was meeting with that afternoon. Maybe some MarTech rep. I had to move quickly."

"But you could have called me from there, couldn't you?"

"What was I supposed to do, jump up and say, 'I have to call my boss.' How does that make me look?"

Before I could answer, there was a knock at the door. It was Kate and her boyfriend, a man of about sixty, richly and elegantly dressed, rumored to be an Argentinian cattle rancher or possibly a Swiss banker.

"Sorry I missed the presentation, Ron. It was unavoidable."

"I know. Too bad. You had to miss the Ficus presentation, too." It just slipped out.

Kate was not fazed. "Hey, Ron, I was asked to join four New World teams. I have a great capacity for work. But don't worry," she said, kissing me on the cheek, "I'm loyal only to you."

"I'm not asking for that."

"Believe it or not, Ficus was approved."

"You're kidding." I was genuinely surprised.

Kate leaned close to me. "Dick has a close friend on the steering committee," she said. "I think he had an inside track."

There were not supposed to be inside tracks in the New World. Andrea arrived with her ex-boyfriend, Mark, a geologist. "We're back together again," she whispered to me. She looked spectacular.

Wesley came alone. Nick Yu was there with his wife, Phyllis with her husband. Only Carlos did not show up, but there could have been a thousand reasons for his absence.

The party was slow getting started, but by the time we got the grill smoking the sun was setting and I started taking food orders and everybody was talking with animation. Kate, clutching her Campari and soda, was talking with Andrea and Phyllis' husband, Barry, an attractive, stolid man.

"Of course we can change!" Kate was saying to Andrea when I joined the group. "Companies can do all kinds of things, make all kinds of amazing turnarounds. I can think of a dozen established companies that got stuck in their ruts and then made fantastic changes. Besides, it's not a choice. We have to do it!"

"But it's so chaotic," said Andrea. "It just feels like we're floundering around. The old FCI had a nice, well-defined structure. And now it's all jelly."

"It was just the jelly you were used to, Andrea. A corporation is amorphous. Everything is always subject to change."

"That's not true in purchasing," said Phyllis. "We haven't changed in years." She laughed.

"You have too changed," said Barry. "You're in a different office now. You're computerized."

"Oh, sure," said Phyllis. "But it's still the same old problems. Those never change. People still fill out purchase orders without all the information. Vendors still present their invoices without a PO number. Managers still blame me for sitting on a purchase order, when it's actually waiting on some executive's desk for approval. That's why I love being on this team. I can say things and people on the team will listen to me. I can do things, and they actually have some effect. We're not used to that in purchasing."

As the evening wore on, I had a chance to talk with everybody. Each one had a FlyingFox issue on his or her mind.

Wesley was worried about the housing material. "I just don't know if we can meet those specs, Ron. At some point you have to say, we've done our due diligence and now it's time to get realistic and rewrite the specs."

"At some point," I agreed. "But not yet. There has to be a solution."

Nick Yu caught up with me in the kitchen.

"Ron, I want to thank you for including me on the FlyingFox team."

"Thank you for suggesting that it be the FlyingFox team."

Nick smiled. "I wonder if I would make the suggestion next time."

"Why do you say that?"

"I am not satisfied with our design so far. It deserves to be better. I don't think it qualifies as Product Delight yet."

"How do you think it could be better?"

"That's the problem. I don't know. My real expertise is the *inside* of these machines."

"Yes."

"But I don't think I have the right skills to make the exterior and the controls elegant enough."

"That's not Wesley's strength either."

"No," said Nick.

I waited to see if Nick would make a suggestion.

"I don't know how much budget flexibility we have," he began, "but I was wondering if we could work with an outside design consultant."

"Have you ever developed a product that way before? With a partner?"

"No, I haven't, but other people in the department have."

"How'd it go?"

"The FCI project manager just wanted the outside firm to be his slaves. He didn't give them enough information to go on, and he didn't want them to really contribute. It got very messy at the end. The project manager just used the firm as a convenient place to attach the blame."

"Which product was it?"

"It never went to market. It died."

I was not encouraged. "How would you go at it differently?"

"It's an attitude more than anything else. I would go into it seeking the best advice and talent we can get, and try to make it a real collaboration."

"Is there any firm you had in mind?"

"Shark."

"Shark?"

"Shark Design."

"Where are they located?"

"Minneapolis."

"Whoa! Shouldn't they at least be in the same state?"

"They're the best," said Nick. "I don't see what difference it makes where they're located as long as we can connect by computer and share CAD drawings."

"What would Zanoski think?"

"He's hard to predict. He could go either way."

By the end of the evening, the talk had turned to FCI lore and tales of Osgood, our founder. Wesley was retelling the age-old story of the Founding. The mythical $3,000 loan. The Garage. The First Product. Osgood designing transistors as he swept the floor.

Jasper had appeared in his tuxedo, post-opera. "This is all apocryphal, you know, Wesley," he said. "Osgood actually was sent to this planet by an advanced civilization, garage and all."

"What was their purpose in doing that?" asked Kate.

"Oh, they were bored up there and thought business looked like fun, so they decided to have a go at it," said Jasper.

"But is that really the garage where he founded FCI?" asked Andrea.

Wesley nodded. "I remember the days when we all worked in that one building. We didn't need a New World then. We didn't need cross-functional teams. Everybody just did what had to be done. And if you needed to talk with somebody, you used the sneakernet."

"Too bad," said Andrea. "It sounds like fun."

There was a moment of silence as everyone pondered the myth of Dr. Osgood and the first Fickies. In that quiet moment, around the gas-fired version of the primordial campfire, I believe we felt more deeply a part of the company than ever before. We were members of a corporate tribe.

That Sunday, still aglow from the success of the Saturday night party, I spent yelling "Pass! Pass it!!" at my soccer team, the Tibias. I coached them brilliantly to a definitive 2–4 loss.

Later, on the way to the promised movie, Kip said, "You know, Dad, we can't hear a word you say from the sidelines during a game. You're running around and yelling and waving your hands, but we have no idea what you want us to do. It's distracting."

I was shocked. "You can't hear me at all?"

"No. Not at all."

"But why didn't you ever tell me?"

"I thought you knew."

"I had no idea." I saw myself from the point of view of a ten-year-old Tibia. A middle-aged man, six foot two, running and desperately waving his arms, his mouth contorted, hair flying.

I wondered if that's how I look at the office.

FOXFILE ENTRY:

- Is there a connection between my role as a youth soccer coach and that of FlyingFox team leader? As a father and a team leader?

Maybe the only genuine parallel is that a business team, like a family, is not a purely rational body. You can have your flow charts and scatter diagrams and time plots right, but if you haven't got the relationships right, forget it.

Part II

26. *The Foxes Find a Home.*

The first Monday of our life as an officially approved New World project was a particularly granular one for me, proceeding in the six- to eight-minute bits of attention to which the modern manager is so accustomed. I called my fellow New World team leaders and discovered that all seven projects (including Ficus, as Kate had reported) had survived the first cut. The battle for resources could only intensify. I tried, without success, to verify whether Ficus had an inside track.

I pondered the housing materials question, and checked with Phyllis to see if other groups had sources for specialty materials we didn't know about. She said she would keep an eye out. "Great party, Ron, by the way."

I talked with Wesley and asked if he could look into the issue of getting R&D connected with engineering, to improve the sharing of data. He promised he would.

I put in a call to Cub in his car, but "the mobile customer had left the service area" and could not be reached. I left him a message to call as soon as possible.

I poked my head in to see Jasper, intending to talk about the rumors, but he was on the phone.

I called Carlos at the North River plant, to see if he was still alive.

"I'm sorry I couldn't make the party," said Carlos. "I had to go out of town rather unexpectedly."

Just before noon, I spoke with Nick Yu about the idea of the design partnership. He had already identified three candidates, and we agreed to visit them over the next ten days. About noon, on my way out to lunch, I passed two men with handcarts rolling a bunch of cartons onto the freight elevator on the mezzanine floor. On an impulse, I went in the direction they had come from, and came upon a large, abandoned conference room. Sun-filled windows on two sides, a couple of forgotten wastebaskets, a flipchart, and a listing secretary's chair missing a wheel.

I grabbed a marker and scribbled in larger letters on the flipchart: ROOM PERMANENTLY RESERVED FOR TEAM FLYINGFOX. A reversion to Old World methods of procurement, perhaps, but it worked. As soon as Andrea saw it, she came up with the name: the Lair.

27. *Swimming With Shark.*

Nick, Andrea, and I constituted what we called the design partner selection task force. We charged ourselves with visiting three candidate design firms, listening to their capabilities presentations, and then making a recommendation to the rest of the team.

We had visited the local firms first, saving Shark, based in Minneapolis, for last. We flew out at six o'clock one morning and arrived at Shark's offices, located in a converted firehouse, well before noon. We entered the reception area, which soared five stories above us. We gazed up at the internal balconies, and were startled to see a large, fuzzy something plummeting toward us. We leaped aside, but the thing—a tawny, furry fox with wings, an adapted child's toy—snapped to a stop and came to rest, bouncing slightly, about ten feet above our heads.

"Hello FlyingFox!" We heard a high, raspy voice and saw a bearish man waving to us from a balcony five stories up. "Welcome to Shark!" he shouted. "I'll be right down!"

Hartmut Horst, Shark's founder, owner, and design guru, was dressed in a black sacky jacket over a multicolor striped T-shirt, sandals, and elegant silk trousers. He led us on a brief tour of Shark's studios, speaking in a European accent that might have been German or Dutch but had a strong strain of British as well. It was a temple of ergonomics and a showplace of technology, with high-powered graphics workstations on many desks. Most impressive, however, was the combination gallery, conference room, and presentation area we reached at tour's end. Examples of Shark's work—some of the most recognizable devices, packages, and machines in America today—were displayed on back-lit shelves at one end of the room.

"Please help yourself," said Hartmut, gesturing to the collection of juices, imported waters, fruit, and pastry arrayed on the conference table. As we did, we were joined by Keith Levy, Hartmut's colleague. He is a man of about thirty, with the striking, dark-featured good looks, quiet voice, and expressive gestures that you might expect from a fine artist, a painter.

"Keith would be working with me on your project, so I asked him to join us today." Keith smiled as he took his place at the table. Andrea looked at him long and carefully. Hartmut leaned forward. "Now, please tell us about FlyingFox."

As we outlined the project for Hartmut and Keith, they asked occasional questions and made comments; we were impressed by their immediate grasp of what we were trying to accomplish. Finally, I turned the conversation to the issue of collaboration.

"One concern we have is how we'll work together, how we'll overcome the issue of distance."

Hartmut waved his hand and smiled. "We do it all the time, here in the States and overseas. It works wonderfully well if you have the proper attitude and the right technology."

"If you put us in touch with your technical people," Keith added, "we can easily determine what is required to connect our computer system with yours."

"What about face-to-face meetings?" asked Andrea.

Hartmut snatched up a remote controller with a flourish. "TV!" Hartmut pressed a button and a wall unit folded away, revealing a videoconferencing setup—a large monitor with a camera fixed above it, flanked by two smaller monitors.

Hartmut slid the controller across the table for me to examine. "No doubt you have many such units at your offices."

"Not in our group, no," I said.

"You can install them very simply, quite inexpensively," said Hartmut.

Purchasing anything new at FCI is seldom simple, and expense was always relative. However, I was intrigued.

"Carlos has a system at North River," Nick reminded me. "We could probably use it."

"Excellent!" Hartmut clapped his hands. "Perhaps we can speak next by video!"

We spent the rest of the morning and into the early afternoon discussing a dozen other issues. Philosophies. Responsibilities. Contracts. Fees. Schedules. During the course of our conversation, the pastries were efficiently cleared away to make room for sandwiches and cookies. By midafternoon, we had concluded our business.

Waiting for the elevator, Andrea noticed that the original brass firepole was still in place. "How wonderful!"

"Yes," said Keith, stepping over the balcony railing and reaching for the pole. "It can come in handy when the pressure gets intense."

He leaped to the pole and slid down to the reception area, then waved up at Andrea.

"Come on, give it a try!" he shouted.

Andrea laughed in delight. "Forget it!"

I had the impression that Keith would gladly have climbed back up just to slide down again for Andrea's enjoyment. As it was, I couldn't remember seeing her so lighthearted and full of energy.

28. *The Partner of Choice.*

Two days later, our selection task force convened in the Lair. We had invited Wesley and Carlos to join us, but only Wesley showed up. On a flipchart page, we wrote COMPANY on the X axis and STRENGTHS AND WEAKNESSES on the Y axis, and set about evaluating our candidates. After an hour, we had eliminated one of the firms. Andrea and Nick strongly favored Shark. Wesley was for the local firm, French Curve. I was neutral.

"I've heard a lot about this guy Hartmut," said Wesley. "I know this type."

"I'm glad you're keeping an open mind," said Andrea. "What do you mean, 'his type'?"

"He's a prima donna. He's not going to be interested in collaborating with us. He won't care what's best for FCI. He won't care about developing a design that fits our manufacturing capabilities. He won't want to reuse existing components or technologies. He's going to want to make the product he wants to make."

"I didn't get that impression from meeting with him," I said.

"Besides," said Andrea, "Keith is the project designer. He's the one we'll be working with most."

"So we get the worst of both worlds. We get the junior guy with not much experience, who we have to bring up to speed. Then we have to deal with a prima donna who I guarantee will come galloping in at the last minute and want to change everything."

Nick shook his head. "Keith isn't inexperienced. Besides, the main issue is the quality of the design. You can't argue that French Curve is as good as Shark. Their stuff is middle of the road, and we're looking for breakthrough design."

"I know. Product Delight," snorted Wesley.

Andrea glared at Wesley. "That is our objective, unless you disagree with Bill Ferry and the steering committee."

"As a matter of fact, I do have a few issues around the mission." Wesley crossed his arms and set his jaw.

"Let's hear about them, Wes," I said.

"Okay. Recycling! We just don't have a housing material to make it a reality. Ferry talks about it. Jasper talks about it. But there is no material we currently work with or know about, for that matter—and that includes French Curve—that has the properties we need and can genuinely be recycled."

"So why aren't you willing to seek help from a new source? Shark didn't seem daunted by the recycling issue."

"But they didn't make any specific suggestions, did they?"

"No," I admitted.

Wesley tried a different tack. "Look, I've worked with French Curve for years now. They're a good solid firm with an excellent track record. They helped us develop FanFare and that's the most successful FCI product of the past five years. If we're going to get FlyingFox out the door in a year, we don't have time to develop a working partnership with a whole new company."

Nick crossed his arms in frustration. If we lost Shark, I was afraid Nick might leave the team.

"Nick? What do you think?" I asked.

Nick hesitated, and then plunged in with a sigh.

"Wesley, I know French Curve, too. I like them, but they do not meet the criteria in this case. They don't have the breakthrough creativity we need. And if we don't have that, FlyingFox is not going to fly."

"I agree strongly," put in Andrea.

Wesley flared at Andrea. "What do you know about it, Andrea? You're a marketing person. You have no idea of the complexities that go into engineering something like this. You think that it's all about color schemes."

"Whoa, Wesley!" I said. "Unfair personal attack on a person of a different discipline."

"Well, she doesn't." Wesley was beyond caring about team etiquette.

Andrea grabbed a marker and flipped to a clean page on the chart.

"I'm sick of the assumption that marketing people only care about irrelevancies, and that engineering is the only thing that really matters." She scribbled the letters *UPA*.

"What does UPA mean?" asked Nick.

"It stands for what Ron said. Unfair Personal Attack on Person of a Different Discipline. We're going to keep track of them from now on." Now Andrea wrote Wesley's name in the left margin, and made a bold hatch mark beside his name.

Wesley retorted. "Better put your name down too, then. You always say that engineers have no creativity. That we're just a bunch of sheet-metal benders."

"I have never said that." Andrea scrawled the date next to Wesley's name, recapped the marker, and chucked it back in the tray with disgust.

"Maybe not, but you believe it."

Andrea rubbed her hands together, as if this act of scoring had improved her mood. "Fine," she said. "Next time you think I step out of line, mark me down."

This amused Wesley. He uncrossed his arms, sat back, and laughed. "I know I'm an engineering bigot, Andrea! I can't help it. My father was an engineer. My daughter is studying to be an engineer. Engineering is the highest calling. It's even above skiing!" Wesley is an avid skier.

Andrea groaned. Nick laughed.

"All right." Wesley shrugged, the light moment breaking down some of his resistance. "Maybe I'm wrong about Hartmut. But I need more convincing."

"What are your concerns?" I asked.

Wesley threw up his hands. "First of all, how are we going to communicate with these guys?"

"Electronically," said Nick.

"But we don't even know if our system's compatible with Shark's. How are we going to transmit documents?"

"They offered to explore the connection issues for us," said Andrea.

Wesley didn't listen. "And what about security? Do you have any idea who their other clients are? Suppose they're working for MarTech! That's how rumors get started, you know."

"We checked for client conflicts at Shark," I reassured Wesley; "there are none."

"Plus we can't have much face-to-face communication with Shark without jumping on a plane. How are we going to work together?"

"Videoconference," Nick blurted out.

Wesley looked at us as if we had completely lost our minds. "You've got to be kidding."

Later that afternoon, Andrea drove out to North River to see their videoconference facility. She called me at the end of the day.

"How'd it go?" I asked.

"Carlos went ballistic."

"What about?"

"He says he wasn't invited to the meeting this morning to select the design firm."

"He was invited."

"He says he wasn't."

"I sent him an E-mail."

"He says he doesn't read E-mail. He gets too much junk."

E-mail bulletin boards had proliferated wildly at FCI in the past couple of years. Travel Tips. Day Care Advice. Soap Opera Digest.

"It was marked urgent and from me."

"Ron, I'm telling you. Carlos says he doesn't read E-mail."

"Great," I said.

"But we can use the videoconference room. On condition

that Carlos is part of the conference and he cross charges you for the time."

"That's fine. And tell him we haven't made our decision yet."

Andrea scoffed. "I'm not saying another word to the guy. You tell him."

I hung up thinking: Carlos won't come to meetings; he doesn't read E-mail; he's too far away from the Lair; how am I supposed to communicate with him? I picked up the phone and punched his number. He answered immediately.

"Carlos."

"Oh." I was surprised to hear his voice. "Just touching base with you. Andrea says you didn't get the E-mail about the meeting."

"I can't stand E-mail, Ron; I have to wade through too much crap. The percentage of useful messages to flame mail, bulletin boards, and ass-covering memos is too low."

"What's the best way for us to communicate?"

"You're using it."

"What if I can't reach you?"

"I'm on a beeper. The call goes right through. I call you right back. I promise. There's no such thing as can't reach me."

"Okay." I must have sounded skeptical.

"Ron." Carlos laughed. "Listen. I'm a rotten writer. I have keyboard phobia. I do much better talking."

The real reason.

"No problem, Carlos," I said. Maybe Kate was right. Peevish was the right word to describe Carlos.

FOXFILE ENTRY:

• Communications are perhaps the single most important aspect of teamwork. And in a large company, the biggest barrier to communications can be an absurdly mechanical one: just making contact.

29. *We Meet by Video.*

We convened, two days later, in the videoconference facility at North River. Carlos and Nick were waiting for us. Hartmut and Keith were already on screen. It was disorienting to walk into a meeting and immediately find yourself on television.

"Good morning!"

"Good morn—" I started to say, but then I realized that Hartmut hadn't finished.

"—stems person," he was saying.

"Sorry," I said.

Hartmut repeated. "We have consulted with our computer systems person. Of course, he is no Prandar," he said, referring to the vaunted FCI software genius, "but he does understand networking very well." Hartmut's voice sounded clipped, his words separated by the dead spaces created by digital transmission.

Carlos leaned forward to me. "There's a little delay in the transmission. It's like talking on a satellite telephone connection overseas."

Andrea was dragging a chair to the table that had been against the wall. "Morning, Keith."

After a second, Keith sat upright and peered toward us.

"Is that you, Andrea?"

"Yeah!" she said, and settled herself into the chair. "I'm—"

"Oh!" Keith cut her off. "I couldn't see you, you were off camera—what?" He stopped, as he heard Andrea begin to speak.

Andrea waited. Keith abruptly pulled his chair closer to the table and his entire face disintegrated into a grid of flesh-colored pixels. Andrea laughed. "You just pixellated."

After a moment, Harmut and Keith laughed. Hartmut leaned forward slowly. "Yes, if you move too quickly, the image degrades. It's best to sit calmly and talk slowly, and then it works fine."

Wesley bustled into the room. "Sorry to be late." He threw his briefcase on the table. He noticed the people on screen now. "Oh!"

I made the introductions. Hartmut and Keith waved, but in delay.

"It's got a delay," Wesley said almost to himself.

"Excuse me?" asked Hartmut.

Wesley spoke louder. "I'm just interested in the delay. Is that simply a function of the satellite?"

"Yes," said Hartmut. "It's also affected by the refresh rate."

Wesley was intrigued that Hartmut, the prima donna designer, could talk about the technical details of videoconferencing.

"Wait till we get high def going across the phone lines," said Wes.

"Yes, we're working with a client in that field."

"Oh, really?" Wesley was intrigued.

"But I'm sure you understand I cannot talk about it further. The project is proprietary, and there is tremendous competition in that area."

"Oh sure," said Wesley, and he turned to me.

Hartmut had managed to show some technical expertise and demonstrate a sensitivity to security issues in the first minute of the conversation. I was impressed by his ability to read our team and respond to our concerns.

"Hartmut, we want to accomplish two things this morning," I began. "First, I wanted Carlos and Wesley to be able to meet the Sharks. That we've done. Two, we want to talk about computer systems. Nick, maybe you could start us off."

"Sure. We're working to make a link between R&D and engineering," said Nick. "Engineering is already linked with manufacturing. And we're asking all three of our potential design partners about how we can link together with them. The goal is to have design, R&D, engineering, and manufacturing on line together."

Carlos pointedly checked his watch. "Could I just break in here to say that we have no more than one hour. The room is booked at ten and satellite time waits for no one."

"I understand," said Hartmut.

Wesley jumped in. "You know, before we talk more about computers, I want to get your impression of FlyingFox."

"We haven't had our hands on a prototype," Keith answered. "And we haven't seen any drawings. We've just gotten written descriptions and a couple of renderings, and the basic technical specs. So I don't think we could give you any kind of intelligent reaction at this point. What we want to do is get together with you and Nick and tear this Fox apart and see if we can work with you to solve any problems you may have. We have some experience with similar products that we'd be happy to share with you."

This was miles away from the prima donna-ish speech that Wesley was expecting. Keith was talking about working together, solving problems—not about dominating FCI's work. He was talking about teamwork.

Wesley shook his head. "I'm sure you've guessed what our toughest problem is."

"The housing material," said Keith mildly.

"Absolutely."

"We have a few thoughts on that issue," said Hartmut.

Carlos broke in. "Remember, that one is also a manufacturing concern. There may be materials that solve the problem in short runs, but we need to produce in high volumes."

Keith paused, waiting for Carlos to finish. "Right. We understand that."

Hartmut looked in my direction. "Do you want to talk about that more now, Ron?"

"I'd like to get back to the connection issue, if we could." I turned to Nick, who plunged into a cascade of computer talk about operating systems and protocols and object-oriented computing and international standards and open systems. Hartmut did most of the talking for Shark, and was impressively computer literate. As we approached ten o'clock, Hartmut checked his watch.

"Perhaps I could summarize for a moment."

"Go ahead," I said, gratefully.

"What we want to do is work with common CAD applications, transmit drawings, and hook into your E-mail network. We want to do that so we can facilitate day-to-day communications, and so we can efficiently manage the process of approvals and revisions. And we need to do it with complete security."

Wesley nodded. "Essentially right."

"I suggest that we work with our computer people—and they with yours—and we'll put together a plan for you.

"That would be useful," I said. "How soon could you put that together?"

"Give us a week," he said.

I looked around the table. Wesley nodded his head and shrugged.

"If you can figure it out that fast, look out EDS."

A second's delay, then Hartmut laughed. After a few parting comments, we signed off. The next group of videoconferencers had already convened in the hallway and were peering in the window.

We talked for a few minutes in the North River lobby.

Andrea asked Wesley, "What do you think?"

Wesley raised his eyebrows. "Hartmut didn't look as weird as I thought he would."

"You should do a stint abroad, Wesley." Carlos pinched at Wesley's coat sleeve, as if examining the fabric. "Then you wouldn't be so concerned about superficial appearances."

"I probably *will* be living abroad, like maybe in Iceland, if FlyingFox doesn't work out."

Carlos laughed.

"He certainly knows his stuff," Nick added.

"We shall see," I said. "Let's make our decision at the next staff meeting." Everyone nodded.

On the way out the door, Wesley turned to me. "Ron, I think we ought to get one of these videoconferencing rigs for the Lair. It's great technology."

30. *Considering the Customer Connection.*

We signed a partnership agreement with Shark Design, which specified their fees (discounted) along with a profit-sharing arrangement that offered them potentially much greater rewards than a straight fee relationship.

Our next major milestone was the second steering committee presentation, after which we would be granted or denied production approval. Judgment Day, as we called it, loomed some twelve weeks ahead, scheduled for mid-September.

With the design and engineering team deeply involved in their work, our focus now could turn to marketing and promotional issues.

"It's time for a focus group," said Kate at the next regular staff meeting. "I'd like to get the agency involved and have them set up two or three sessions over the next several weeks."

"Sessions to do what?" asked Nick.

"Show the prototype," said Kate. "Get some reaction from honest-to-god real customers."

"It's too early," said Nick. "FlyingFox isn't ready."

"We need some initial feedback. It's never too early for that."

Nick protested. "But we're still not there on one of the most important aspects of the product to the customer. The exterior—the housing, the packaging, and the controls."

The team had had two demonstrations of FlyingFox capabilities. It still didn't look like much, but it functioned well. Kate, at both demos, had seemed underwhelmed.

"When *are* you going to be there?" asked Kate. "You've been saying this since our first meeting."

Wesley came to Nick's defense. "We're exploring several possibilities, Kate."

"We can't wait forever, Wesley. I'm supposed to be the voice of the customer here. But I can't do that without hearing a few customers speak for themselves. I want to know what some real people like about the product, what they don't like, and what they think is missing."

The speaker phone crackled. We heard Cub's voice above distant road noise. "Kate, you don't need a focus group to find that out. I can tell you right now."

"I'm talking about systematic research into customer concerns, Cub."

"There's no such thing as systematic when it comes to customers, Kate."

"The hell there isn't."

"Don't you have any faith in FlyingFox?"

Kate considered her response for a moment. "Well, to tell you the truth, based on the demos I've seen so far, I think we've got more of a dog on our hands than a fox. That's why we've got to get this thing out into the field and hope for all our sakes that I'm wrong."

The room fell silent. This was the first time that Kate—anyone, for that matter—had expressed such strong and negative opinions about our prospects. I started to say something, but Andrea was already reacting.

"Why haven't you said this before, Kate?" Andrea asked.

Kate mimicked Nick. "It was too early. I wanted to give these guys a chance to pull the thing together. But now we're running out of time, and, in my opinion, we're not even close to Product Delight. What we've got is a lot of wishful thinking in a sheet-metal box that talks."

"Wait a minute." Wesley was not going to let this pass by. "That's an Unfair Personal Attack of the first water. I don't think you get what this product is all about, Kate. I don't think you understand what an achievement it is already."

"Maybe I don't. But if I don't get it, will the customer?" she responded.

"The customers will get it, because you're going to help them get it. Isn't that what marketing and advertising are all about?"

"No, it's not. It's not about making something up that isn't there. It's about bringing out qualities that already exist, putting the product in the best light, making it memorable, attractive, *valuable* in the eyes of the customer. Contrary to popular opinion, we only create vaporware when we're given vaporware to work with."

Wesley obviously had had this discussion many times before. "Okay, but when you're looking for a breakthrough product, you can't ask the customer to assess its value. People respond best initially to designs they know and recognize. Our job with FlyingFox is to *lead* them, not deliver another safe, me-too product that has immediate familiarity but that they're going to get bored with in the first year."

"That's just engineering rationalization for saying the customer is too stupid to understand the genius of your screwy design. So, even if the product bombs, you can say to yourselves, oh poor us, they just didn't understand. We were way ahead of our time."

I stepped in. "Okay. Slow down. Let's try to avoid the

sniping and get back to the original question. Kate has expressed some concerns—"

Wesley snorted at the mildness of the term "concerns."

"—some concerns about the viability of FlyingFox. Now, these concerns are not necessarily new to us. The question is, is it time to start getting some outside opinions? And, if so, are focus groups the best way to go?"

"I'll tell you," said Carlos, now pacing around the room. "I don't think it's wise to do any kind of focus group or beta-site testing this early. For two reasons. One, you're asking for a leak. You're just begging for someone to spill the beans to one of our competitors."

Kate interrupted him. "Nonsense. We can do a focus group without—"

"If I could finish," said Carlos, interrupting right back. "And number two, which is the most important, is that we don't even have a production go-ahead from our own management. If the results are bad from the focus group, then they could affect our ability to get FlyingFox approved."

"On the other hand," said Kate, her voice rising in intensity, "if we can get some positive feedback from customers it'll *help* with the steering committee."

"I say wait," concluded Carlos and leaned against the wall.

"What about you, Cub?" I called into the speaker phone.

"Uh, I don't think it really matters. I rely on what my customers tell me every day. I'm in touch with them all the time. My experience is that people lie in focus groups, anyway. They say what they think they're supposed to say. So I don't think it makes any difference. It won't to me anyway."

"Wait a minute," cut in Kate. "The focus group is just one of the tools of the modern marketing professional. Okay, it has its limitations, but it provides some hard data to add to your gut feelings and all the other information we gather. What if I were to suggest to you that you really didn't need to take your customers to lunch, Cub, because they tend to say things they don't mean while eating? That's not the only way you gather information, but it's one of the ways, and you use your intelligence and experience to interpret the results. That's all I'm suggesting."

In the Old World, this would never have come to a discussion because there would have been no forum for it. Marketing or the product managers always did focus groups. And the design team always resisted them. Marketing always put together a neat report summarizing the results. And the design team usually disputed the meaning of the results.

Our discussion went on for some time but ended without a decision. Kate agreed to discuss it further with me, Wesley, and Nick.

We moved on to a discussion of the steering committee presentation. It was planned as a major, three-day off-site meeting, at which all the New World teams would make presentations the first day, receive feedback the second, and then analyze and review the reactions on the third.

If FlyingFox was approved, our next milestone would be the most exciting one of all: product launch.

If FlyingFox was killed . . . well, although that possibility lurked in the back of our minds, we couldn't bring ourselves to talk about it. Even the most modern and technologically sophisticated of organizations has its superstitions. Ours was that to talk about failure was to improve its chances of occurring.

31. *Fox Talk.*

FOXFILE ENTRY:

The partnership with Shark brought forward the issue of the role of technology, particularly information technology (IT), in the functioning of the team.

- E-mail. A commonplace. No more extraordinary today than the mailroom of yesterday, though much more immediate. Without it, however, we could not function.

- Voice mail. Benefits: eliminates telephone tag. Problems: eliminates give-and-take conversations. Dialogue becomes a succession of monologues.

- Videoconferencing. Now an accepted meeting substitute for us. Reduces travel time. Enhances our ability to work with distant partners/colleagues. Which means we can always seek out the best people for the job, wherever they may be. Cost: probably no increase, if you factor in reduced travel expenses.

Videoconferencing also gave us our first test of Jasper's commitment to our team. He approved purchase of a system for the Lair.

- Design and drafting. Computers simplify the job of creating drawings, making changes, and getting approvals. You can do more iterations, and thus try out more ideas. Everybody is kept up to date. You have better security. Whether this actually reduces the length of the development process remains to be seen.

- Sharing information. In the Old World, power often was attained and maintained by hoarding information. In the New World, teamwork depends on sharing information. We established a Team FlyingFox database. It contains minutes of all meetings. All team correspondence. And a file on MarTech, containing all information, scanned-in articles, etc.

- Gaps. We still have a few gaps, however. Cub, and the entire sales force really, is out in the wilderness, virtually unconnected. And there is no connection between Team FlyingFox and the financial controls of the company. I diligently prepare my reports and make forecasts using our departmental financial software and send them on to the team's financial adviser. But there is no connection between it and the financial database that is the company's fiscal engine: sales data, purchasing, and cost information and the like.

Computer suppliers love to talk about how their solutions can provide a competitive advantage to our company. I have a gut feeling that this is sometimes true, but it is an awfully difficult thing to measure.

32. *We Encounter Trouble.*

As we got closer and closer to Judgment Day, I was usually to be found in my office by seven in the morning. Carlos had discovered my early-morning habits, being a six o'clock person himself, and liked to call me then if he needed to talk.

"Ron, we've got a problem and I don't think our group can solve it. We need some direction from you before we waste much more time going around in circles."

"Tell me about it." I tried to keep my voice from betraying my anxiety.

"We just can't produce FlyingFox within the costs we're talking about and the time deadline, and meet all the criteria of Product Delight."

"Is it because of the housing material problem?"

"Yeah. Wesley and Nick were here until late last night, with a couple of the R&D guys, some of my people, and Keith from Shark, and we went round and round and ended up nowhere."

"What are the issues?"

"They're what they've been from the beginning, Ron." I heard exasperation, annoyance, and fatigue. "The plastic we normally would use for a product like this doesn't have the cosmetic properties we need. The material with the best cosmetics doesn't have the structural strength we're after. And the only composite material that provides both you can't recycle, and is too hard to work anyway. We've tried mixing and altering, changing cycle times, doing all kinds of tricks. Nothing works."

"What are the alternatives?"

"We could go one of two ways, I think. First, we could simply argue to the steering committee that we can't deliver the recyclability."

"Or?"

"The other possibility is to get Shark to back off on some of their cosmetic requirements. I'm beginning to think this partnership approach isn't such a good idea. Those people are too demanding. I know we're after quality, I know we're looking for innovation and breakthrough. But these guys don't like to compromise. I'm beginning to think Wesley was right. There's some prima donna behavior going on."

"Where do you stand right now?"

"I can't commit any more time and resources to making prototype after prototype and running test after test chasing this holy grail of Product Delight. I'm at the end of my rope. Something has to give."

This was not just peevishness. Carlos was frustrated and feeling abused.

"Let me think about this, and talk to the others. I'll get back to you."

"Sure, but Ron, we've got very little time to build something that will convince the steering committee. Some of the people on that committee really know their stuff, and we can't put anything over on them. Plus, I'm not going to put my reputation on the line by walking in there with some half-assed model that looks like a junior high school kid made it in shop."

"I understand, and I won't put you in that position. I'll get back to you."

"You know where to find me."

Before I had a chance to think about Carlos, I got the second call, this one from Zanoski.

"Ron." The voice was neutral, completely without affect.

"Good morning, Doctor."

"I'm sorry, but I cannot allow Nick to work on your project any further."

"Doctor, as we discussed before, Nick has chosen to participate—"

"Yes," said Zanoski, "but as I told you before, if I saw any disintegration of his performance I would have to step in."

"And have you seen such evidence?"

"That is why I am calling you. I was in early this morning, checking on an experiment before I met with a visitor. Nick was supposed to have logged some data for me before going home last night, but when I came in, I discovered that he had not done so. Nick told me he would leave it on my desk, but it wasn't there, so I went to see if he had left it in his area instead. I found Nick asleep on the floor of his office. He obviously had not been home last night. When I woke him up, he was in a daze and said he had been unable to log the data because he was meeting at North River until well after midnight."

"That's unfortunate," I said.

"It is more than unfortunate. It jeopardized the validity of an important experiment, and it is unprofessional behavior besides. This is what I feared would happen from the beginning, and now I simply must pull him off your project."

"Why don't we talk with Nick together."

"There is nothing to talk about."

"I'm sure you can appreciate that Nick plays a crucial role on this New World team. He would be difficult to replace at this point."

"I understand that, but you understood the risks from the beginning. Now I must go. My visitor has arrived."

Zanoski hung up. I called Nick's office, but was transferred into voice mail. I tried him at home and got his wife. He had called her, but had not made it home last night. She thought he was with Keith from Shark Design, maybe at his hotel. I called the hotel and got through to Keith's room. Not in. I slammed down the phone. It rang immediately.

"Hi, Ron, it's Nick. I'm in the Lair with Keith. Can you come down?"

"I'll be right there." Andrea was just arriving, so I grabbed her and we walked down together. I told her about the developments of the morning so far.

"What are we going to do?"

"I don't know."

In the Lair, Nick and Keith were surrounded by drawings and documents. They looked rumpled, harried, tired, and stressed.

"I just wanted to warn you—" Nick began.

"I've already heard from both Carlos and Zanoski."

"Why Zanoski?" Nick seemed confused.

"He said you failed to record some data because you were at North River last night, and that he wanted you off FlyingFox."

"But I got another guy in the department to do it. And I handed the data to Zanoski this morning."

"He didn't tell me that."

"Did he say he didn't get that data?"

"No. He just said the experiment was jeopardized."

"It wasn't."

The phone buzzed.

"Ron, what's going on out there?" It was Hartmut.

"What do you mean?"

"I was in a conference call this morning with Wesley and Carlos. They're telling me that I am being inflexible and that they cannot create what we have developed—developed together. Why wasn't Nick in that call? Why weren't you? What is going on?"

"I didn't know they had called you, Hartmut. All I know is that Carlos is concerned about meeting all the specs, and is particularly worried about the housing material issue. He's saying that you're refusing to compromise on changes."

"Do you know why he's saying that?" Hartmut sounded

genuinely angry and disturbed. "Wesley and his people have been making changes to the drawings, changes that affect appearance and user functionality, without discussing them with us. We agreed that they would make only those changes that would affect internal structure or manufacturing tooling. But they have made two important changes that significantly affect the appearance of FlyingFox—for the worse—and make it less easy to use. This we cannot tolerate. They must be discussed with us. It's a mockery of the work we have done!"

"Okay, Hartmut. Let me investigate a bit further on this end and we'll be back in touch."

As soon as I hung up, the phone buzzed again. Cub, in his car.

"Ron, the leaks are getting bigger!"

"What have you heard?"

"I had dinner with a guy from one of our biggest customers last night."

"Yes?"

"Around about dessert, which I never eat, of course, except for maybe a bit of fruit sometimes, he said, 'So what's this I hear about a new FCI office machine, with voice activation, designed by that Shark guy, Hartmut whoever?' I asked him where he'd heard this ridiculous rumor and he said he'd heard it from somebody in their marketing department."

"Did he know anything more?"

"He said the rumor was that we were scrambling to catch up with MarTech's product and that we were shooting for launch within four to six months."

"I hope you told him that we never scramble to catch up with MarTech."

"Has Kate run any focus groups without telling anybody?"

"She wouldn't do that," I said, knowing that she was quite capable of doing just that, "but I'll talk to her."

"Better do it soon. If these people know, there's no telling who else knows."

I hung up and looked at Andrea. "We need a staff meeting before Wednesday. Would you see if we can get everybody in here on Monday? Hartmut, too."

"Yes, boss, anything you say, boss," she said.

FOXFILE ENTRY:

• The quaint phrase "storming" is what the experts use to describe the phase of team life we now find ourselves in. Carlos threatening to quit. Nick in jeopardy. Hartmut confused. Rampant rumors. Cross communications. Me out of the loop.

Perhaps one of the clearest tests of a team is how it responds to crises of this sort. I have read that in difficult times, people tend to revert to old patterns. In particular, nervous leaders (who may have just begun to shed their Old World ways) sometimes respond to crisis by reverting to boss mode and grabbing back the reins of authority from newly empowered workers. The unfortunate result is that trust is broken and the team's progress is set back.

I did not have that urge. Instead, when we faced the loss of an important team member and a possible major redesign of the product, I did not feel the specter of Captain Courageous looming up within me. Nor did I run to Jasper. I gathered as much information as I could and then turned to my best resource: the team.

33. *We Are Delivered of a Solution.*

Hartmut flew in early Monday morning. Cub motored (his word) down from a lakeside cabin he visited with his family every weekend. Keith, already in town, stayed over the weekend at Andrea's. (I had watched as the two had become close friends in the past several weeks. I didn't ask about Mark any more.) Kate, at my urging, postponed a planned trip until later in the day. Nick decided to sneak out of R&D without Zanoski noticing. Wesley brought along two associates. Steadfast Phyllis was there. At nine-thirty, as the meeting was due to start, only one key player was missing—Carlos.

Just as I was bringing the meeting to order, there was a tap at the Lair door and Nelson Favreaux appeared.

"Carlos can't make it," said Nelson. "He asked me to sit in."

This did not please me. Carlos' call had been one of the precipitators of this meeting. "Where is he?" I asked.

"I'm not sure. I think he's traveling. He called me from the road." Nelson sat and tried to be inconspicuous.

"Can we get him on the line? Is he somewhere he can talk?"

"No. He said he was going into a meeting and couldn't be disturbed."

I considered Nelson carefully for the first time. He was a quiet, even diffident fellow, given to dressing in short-sleeved polo shirts that showed off his well-muscled arms. He was not necessarily the man I would have chosen to be our team member but now, by default, he was. I decided that if Carlos trusted him, he must have more to offer than he generally displayed.

"Okay," I began. "We have two serious conflicts that we have to resolve soon, if we're going to have a chance at getting production approval at Judgment Day."

I looked around at the assembled faces and realized that in the Old World, I would not have been bringing these issues before a group like this. I wouldn't have had a group like this to help, at all. Instead, I would have been wrestling with the problems myself—or delegating, that is to say dumping, them on someone—and trying to find a way to appease every faction without alienating any other. Here, as a team, we were focusing on the result, a successful product, rather than trying to affix blame or avoid it. I grabbed a marker and riffled to a clean page on the flipchart.

"Issue number one: Nick's involvement. Dr. Zanoski feels that Nick is too pressed to contribute to other projects. I'm wondering," I said, looking at Wesley and Keith, "if we can reduce Nick's involvement on the project and still keep him involved." Nick and I had agreed to open this issue up for general discussion.

Everyone started to talk at once. I held up my hand. "And, just so we have an agenda, issue number two is the housing material. Carlos is telling me that he thinks we can't meet all the specs for material characteristics of Product Delight, and that we have to make a serious program change of some kind."

Two hours of discussion followed. By eleven-thirty we had explored a hundred solutions and chosen none. Then, during a lull in the tumult, Phyllis tentatively raised her hand.

"Phyllis," I said, nodding at her, "what's on your mind?"

"Has anyone heard of FungiFlex?" she asked mildly.

Blank stares all around. Was this an irrelevancy?

"No, Phyllis. What is FungiFlex?"

"It's a plastic material. I think it could solve both our problems."

The stares turned to curiosity and disbelief.

"How so?"

"Well," Phyllis smoothed her skirt, as if preparing to tell a fascinating bedtime story to a favorite grandchild. "I was in a meeting with my boss in purchasing. She had volunteered me again." Phyllis shook her head and chuckled. "This time she wanted me to take over the responsibilities for someone in our department who's on extended medical leave."

"Yes?" I was impatient with Phyllis, sure she was digressing.

"We were just getting started when Dr. Zanoski came in. He didn't have an appointment, but he pretty much insisted on talking with my boss right then and there."

Everyone became more attentive when Phyllis mentioned Zanoski.

"Of course he ignored me, because, you know, who am I but a purchasing agent. And a woman."

Uneasy laughter.

"Well." Phyllis folded her hands and plunked them in her lap. "He wanted to know if we had a source for purchasing liquid crystals."

Nick looked perplexed. "Why wouldn't he buy them through our regular source?"

"He said he needed to buy much larger quantities than usual and wanted to get some competitive bids."

This still seemed like a digression, but she had our complete attention.

"My boss asked him about specifications and Dr. Zanoski gave her a sheet of specs. Then she asked what the crystals were for."

Phyllis paused, dramatically.

"He said, 'It's for a new plastic material we've been experimenting with.' My boss said, 'Oh, really. I haven't heard about it. What is it?' Then Zanoski looked at me again, probably to make sure I really *was* a nobody," continued Phyllis, "and I guess he decided I was. 'We've been working on it about four years now,' he said. 'It's a thermoplastic composite, reinforced with liquid crystals. It's called FungiFlex.' 'Oh,' asked my boss, 'what's the advantage of that?' "

Phyllis paused once again, squeezing the story for every ounce of value.

"Zanoski said, 'It's very strong. Very workable. And has a good surface finish.' " Phyllis' voice dropped lower. "And this is the best part," she said. "He said, 'Plus, FungiFlex can be reused up to five times. You could get fifty years of use out of this material. That's as close to a completely recyclable plastic material as you can get.' "

Phyllis let the impact of her story sink in. Whether FungiFlex was the answer to our problems or not, I realized we had been overlooking one of the most valuable resources at FCI, Dr. Zanoski himself, precisely because we were involved in a turf dispute of the type I had worked so hard to discourage. I had never brought up the material issue with him, never thought of doing so. Could it be possible, I wondered, that Zanoski was being uncooperative, not out of spite or obstinacy, but because he wanted to be consulted? Could it be possible that he was feeling slighted, even hurt?

I turned to Nick. "Did you ever discuss the material issue with Zanoski?"

"Are you kidding? I've never discussed FlyingFox with him at all. I was afraid to bring it up."

"So," continued Phyllis, reveling in her moment. "I thought, why not make FlyingFox out of FungiFlex? We'd have the material we need. Zanoski probably would be happy too, and he might be more willing to let Nick stay involved."

We all looked at Phyllis as if she were our savior. I thought, if cross-functional eavesdropping is a hidden benefit of team-work, then we had better take advantage of it.

Even now, when some acute problem faces us and none of the traditional solutions is working, someone will say, "What we need here is a FungiFlex." It is FlyingFox shorthand for a solution that is right before our eyes, that solves more than one problem, and does so in a way we never would have expected.

34. *The Zanoski Factor.*

Andrea and Nick took Hartmut and Keith on a tour of FCI, and I was lucky enough to find Zanoski in his office when I telephoned.

"I have not changed my mind about Nick's involvement," he said over the phone.

"I understand. That's not what I want to discuss."

"What's on your mind then?"

"Something I hope will intrigue you," I said. He agreed to meet me late in the afternoon.

As I approached Zanoski's office I tried to visualize him in a different way. I did my best to exorcise the image of Dr. Z, the predatory genius, sitting atop his R&D nest like a hawk, ready to strike at any invader who might threaten his precious projects. But I wasn't sure what image to replace it with. How did he see himself and his position? He was so guarded and complete in himself that it was difficult to tell.

Zanoski was dressed in a suit of the finest summer-weight wool, a complex and subtle blend of olives and grays that fell gracefully around his tall, spare frame.

"Come in, Ron." Why is it that when old-world Europeans call Americans by their first name it always sounds loud and awkward? Like calling your father-in-law "Bill" for the first time, or addressing a child you don't like much.

"Thank you for seeing me, Doctor." He inclined his head and motioned me into his office. Zanoski was cool, distracted. As we sat, Dr. Z pressed two well-manicured fingers to an eyebrow as if under stress.

"Now," he said, and stopped, expecting me to begin.

I resorted to flattery as an opening gambit. "Congratulations on the conference results." The Doctor was chairman of an international technical standards committee, which had recently gotten some positive coverage in the trade press. Zanoski brightened. A crooked smile bloomed.

"Yes! You can imagine what it is like trying to get a consortium of governments and industries to agree on these things. It is very difficult."

I had never considered Zanoski's work on these conferences as real work, but rather thought of his jetting off to Zurich and Seoul and Kauai as so much junketing cum public relations.

"Now," said Zanoski, as if aware that I was trying the chat-and-flatter approach to problem resolution. "About Nick."

I wanted the first comment on this. "Yes, Dr. Zanoski." I leaned forward, wanting to connect with him. "I realize I haven't managed Nick's involvement well from your point of view. But I'm sure you can appreciate this cross-functional team approach is a new process for all of us. It may not be as complex as getting governments to agree, but we are under considerable pressure."

Zanoski pressed his fingers tighter to his brow. "Yes, of course, I understand."

"And I appreciate that you've been operating with reduced staff and reduced resources and that Nick is a valuable asset to your department."

Zanoski shrugged as if to say, "I can take it."

"When I began putting the team together I simply focused on getting the best people I could, and I didn't consult you properly about Nick." I couldn't believe I was apologizing to Zanoski, but, at the same time, I now genuinely saw that in putting together my New World team I may have been using Old World methods. Grab the resources you want and grab them first. The old rule was: It's always easier to beg forgiveness than to seek permission. I'm not sure that rule applies in the New World.

"He is a talented member of my staff," said Zanoski, accepting my apology obliquely. "I may not be the kind of manager who is constantly praising his people. I find that childish. However, I do value him. In fact, I need him. Particularly as I spend so much of my time on ambassadorial functions. Believe me, I would be just as happy to be in the labs more often."

"But what I regret more," I continued, "is that by alienating you, we have not able to consult with you. We are facing some terribly difficult issues with FlyingFox and we need the best ideas we can muster. We'd be grateful if you could spend some time working with us."

Zanoski's fingers came off the brow. Clearly, for all his jet-setting, for all his hectic scheduling, this was a man who liked to be needed. He could not refuse a plea for help.

"What sort of problems are you having?" he asked, his tone softening.

I talked briefly about the issues we were trying to resolve, leaving the material question for last. I could not bring myself to tell him that Phyllis, that insignificant purchasing lady in the cardigan sweater, had overheard him talking about FungiFlex.

"The critical issue, however, is the housing material. Perhaps you've seen the specs for it?" Nick routinely reported to Zanoski about FlyingFox in written memoranda, but we had no idea whether he actually read them.

"Of course I have seen Nick's reports," said Zanoski. "Yes, the material poses an interesting challenge." Dr. Z now disappeared into his own thoughts for a moment. He leaned back and stared at the wall behind me.

"I didn't know that you had looked at the reports," I said, devising a way to get to FungiFlex obliquely. "I assumed you were too busy with your own development projects."

Zanoski gave me a look I couldn't interpret.

"Yes. I am." He seemed to dismiss his reservations. He leaned forward. "And, strangely enough, I think there may be some connection between my current efforts and your FlyingFox."

"Oh really?" I felt his excitement rising, as well as my own.

"This, please, is between you and me."

"Of course."

"I have been very frustrated at our ability to get new products out of development and onto the market. I sometimes think that people suspect me of living in an ivory tower and looking down my nose at the dirty world of commerce. That's absurd. I feel the frustration more than anyone, and bear the greatest responsibility of all, for our inability to get more new technologies and systems into the marketplace."

"I understand that."

"Perhaps what you do not know is that as part of the New World program, while you were being asked to form your teams I was also being pressured by Ferry to speed up our process."

"I see."

130

"Now, Ron." Zanoski became conspiratorial; he leaned urgently toward me on his couch.

"Perhaps you have heard through the rumor mill that we've been working on a new material. It is a breakthrough material, and it may very well have the properties you need for FlyingFox. It is now ready to go. However, my dilemma has been to find the best product with which to launch it."

"Yes. And have you found one?"

Zanoski sat back again. He seemed disturbed, and he spoke slowly now.

"No. You see, we went through a similar experience some eight years ago."

"That was before my time."

"At that time we had developed another new material, called F-Six. It was extremely promising, and we decided to introduce it in a rather risky but potentially exciting new product the retail group had developed. Unfortunately, the product was a complete failure and many of its flaws were unfairly blamed on the F-Six material. Then, within three months, a competitor introduced a material similar to our F-Six and it was tremendously successful. Although we had gotten to market first with the material, they had gotten to market best. It's an example of the validity of Ferry's 'early to market.' The result is that, today, we are the number three supplier of the F-Six material worldwide. Our competitor's material is still number one, in a market we should have owned."

"So you want to be sure to link your new material with a winning product."

"Exactly."

"But do you think this new material—"

"It's called FungiFlex. Or F-Flex, for short."

"Do you think that F-Flex could work for FlyingFox?"

"Without a doubt. It has superb cosmetic properties."

"Do you think manufacturing can work with it?"

"It will make their lives easier."

"And it's recyclable?"

"F-Flex retains enough of its properties so it can be reused in successively less demanding applications at least five times. That, today, is virtually the definition of recycling."

I said nothing, waiting for him to make his offer, to join us.

"If F-Flex takes off," he said, pensively, "I think you would start to see a cascade of new ideas emerging from this department."

"Emil," I said, "we would be greatly honored if you would work with the FlyingFox team. Whatever amount of time you can offer us."

Zanoski smiled. Suddenly, he was full of energy. He clapped his hands and jumped off the couch. "Done!" he said. He extended his hand to me.

"What about Nick?" I asked, seizing the moment.

Zanoski clicked his tongue. "Ah! He's young. He can handle the workload. I remember working sixteen-hour days in the lab when I was his age."

When I returned from Zanoski's, I found Keith and Andrea in the Lair, deep in a discussion of the Bauhaus influence on industrial design.

"I think we've got a solution to the material problem," I announced and explained about Zanoski and F-Flex.

Andrea was ecstatic. "That's fabulous!" she yelped, grabbing Keith's arm in delight. "You have to do something very nice for Phyllis, Ron. She deserves a huge reward."

"What do you suppose she'd like?"

"Write her a note," said Andrea. "I think that's what would mean the most to her."

"You don't think we should buy her something?"

"No," said Andrea. "That's not the point. That poor lady has been slaving away in purchasing for years now, and I bet she hasn't gotten a word of praise in all those years. All she gets is 'Phyllis, where's that PO? Phyllis, can't you get a better price on those units? Phyllis, why the hell does this thing cost so much?' Write her a note, and put a little heart into it."

"But we don't really know if F-Flex is going to work."

"Ron, the lady took a risk, put herself out on a limb for old Team FlyingFox. Give her a medal!"

"You're right," I said, and went dutifully to my desk.

"Come on, Keith," said Andrea. "Let's get some lunch and let Ron write."

Keith grabbed his portfolio. "I have a couple of other concepts for the pod design that I want to show you, too."

Off they went, eagerly picking up their discussion of the Bauhaus where they had left off a few moments ago.

Here is what I wrote:

> Phyllis,
>
> Thank you for speaking up in the team meeting today and suggesting what sounds like a promising solution to our current problems. I spoke with Dr. Zanoski (without letting on that I'd heard about Fungi-Flex), and he volunteered the information of his own accord. This morning he represented a problem for us. Now he's an important ally—thanks to you.
>
> Phyllis, I want you to know that when I first approached you, I was skeptical about having a purchasing person on the team. I don't need to tell you how marketing people generally view purchasing folk. But you have become a valued member of our team. I respect your abilities and appreciate your contributions.
>
> Whatever happens with F-Flex and the Fox, please know that I am honored to be working with you.
>
> Best,
> Ron

It felt corny, but it was honestly felt. I decided not to put the note in E-mail. I didn't fax it to her. I wrote it on a sheet of stationery (I considered borrowing Jasper's Mont Blanc, but settled for my own Cross ballpoint), folded it neatly into an envelope, wrote her name in my best hand, and strolled down to the third floor. I left the envelope on her desk, propped against the pump dispenser of pink hand lotion.

FOXFILE ENTRY:

- The fountain pen (or the pencil, for that matter) is a communications technology. In some cases, it enables teamwork more effectively than the most powerful desktop workstation.

The emergence of the Phyllises of FCI is the essence of the New World teams. If we could get everyone in the organization to be a Phyllis—to pay attention, feel a part of the effort, make a contribution—the possibilities are enormous.

35. *We Appeal to Kate.*

With the material issue under control for the time being, and Nick back on the job—with Zanoski as guidance counselor, I hoped, and not dictator—I purposely made myself scarce to let the design team work without me gazing nervously over their shoulders.

I returned my attention to the world of the customer, hoping we weren't going to come to market too late or with a product that nobody wanted. The electronic MARTECH file was brimming with rumors and news tidbits. From what I could tell, we were slightly ahead of them and our product was better conceived. But it was impossible to know for sure.

The other pressing issue was Kate. Since she had so forcefully expressed concerns about the worth of FlyingFox, she had been traveling and busy on other projects and we had not communicated except for a couple of routine E-mails. Now, with the appearance of FungiFlex and Zanoski's involvement, I thought it was time to get our relationship back on track. I asked her to join Cub and me for lunch at the same restaurant where Andrea and I had eaten earlier. We sat outside and Kate seemed to soften slightly in the sunlight. She ordered a Campari and soda, Cub drank beer. I stuck with water.

I began by telling Cub and Kate about our progress with F-Flex. "You're going to see a whole different product, next prototype. F-Flex will make some physical and cosmetic things possible that we couldn't achieve with any other material."

Kate was pleased, but not won over. "I repeat my standard question. Do you think the customer will notice?"

"Yes. F-Flex has a special look and texture to it. It's like those new book jackets that are almost like waxed paper. But very durable. Easy to clean. Takes colors well." Zanoski had shown me some samples of other F-Flex applications at the end of our visit, and I had fallen in love with the stuff—if a person can fall in love with a plastic composite.

"What about Zanoski? Did you manage to smooth his feathers?"

"Yes, he's even going to work with us."

Kate turned to me so sharply I thought I heard her neck crack.

"Zanoski is on board with FlyingFox?"

"Why does that surprise you so?"

Kate's eyes narrowed. "That changes everything."

"Yes, it helps."

"No, I mean that's a signal. I don't care how under fire the guy is, he still has tremendous clout. If he's behind FlyingFox, it'll get done."

It was difficult not to take this comment as a direct insult to my abilities to manage FlyingFox. Zanoski still had traditional FCI power, in Kate's eyes, and I was just a middle manager/coach. "I thought it was the customer whose opinion you were concerned with."

"Don't be peevish, Ron," said Kate. "I'm a realist. There's no point fretting about the customer if the product isn't even going to get out the door."

"Is that what you expected?"

"Ron, look at it from my point of view. FCI has a marketing and advertising war chest that is only so large. My group serves all the U.S. groups, not just Technology Systems. As you know, I'm being inundated by requests for help by seven New World teams, each of whom thinks its product should get the biggest launch in FCI history. I have to pick and choose and help rank which ones FCI should put the most resources into."

This was not how I would have defined Kate's role on Team FlyingFox. "But the groups are operating in different markets and targeting different customers," I said. "Why can't all the New World products get the kind of attention they deserve?"

"I told you: resources. Besides, not all of them deserve much attention. If we go out and scream too loudly about a product that turns out to be a total loser—the Ficus dog, for example—we all look like jerks. Some products do better if you slip them quietly into the marketplace. You know, with some trade show exposure or some strategically placed PR. But not a big, full-blown campaign."

"How does Zanoski's involvement affect promotion?"

Kate shook her head, exasperated. "Ron, come on. There are politics to be played here. If Zanoski is behind FlyingFox, he's going to make sure the resources get freed up. He can lever the bucks out of the steering committee. And that'll give my people the freedom to perform at their best."

"So *you* look good."

"Of course I want to look good. But the goodness gets shared with you and FlyingFox, too."

"Kate, I'm in charge of this budget. Jasper and I are the guys who allocate the resources. Zanoski is just an adviser."

Kate put her hand on my forearm and wrinkled her nose at me. "I know, Ronnie. I know you are. But you can't deny that if Zanoski is with us, you're probably going to be able to access more money than you would have otherwise."

She was patronizing me. My first impulse was to slug her, but I decided that physical violence had no role in effective teamwork. What was most annoying to me was that while I played the team game, Kate went right on building and protecting her power base.

"Kate. I'm willing to bet you right now that FlyingFox is going to be a winner, and that it won't be because Zanoski pulls rank. It'll be because the team makes it happen."

"Okay, Ron," said Kate, amused. "What do you bet?"

"If you win, you can have my office," I said. Cub gasped.

"Done," said Kate. "And if *you* win?"

"I get to keep it."

Kate shook her head and extended her hand. "Of course, I don't know how the hell you're going to prove that teamwork had anything to with the product's success."

"I won't try. I'll leave it up to you to make the judgment. We'll talk after the thing is launched and out there, and I'll let you decide."

Kate snorted. "You really are committed to FlyingFox, aren't you?"

"Yes, I am," I said, not knowing why I felt so committed or so willing to challenge her. Was I beginning to develop genuine loyalty to the team? Kate looked at me with new respect.

"All right, Ronnie. It's a deal."

We studied the menu for a moment and I debated how to bring up the subject of the rumors.

"Now, what the hell are we going to do about these rumors flying around?" Kate asked, folding the menu decisively and reaching for her drink. "How do you think this stuff is getting leaked?"

Cub breathed a sigh of relief. "We thought you were leaking it," he said, ingenuously.

Kate let out a guffaw loud enough to attract the attention of a party of Fickies dining at the adjacent table. "Why would I do that, you idiot?"

"Well," said Cub, "well. . ."

"That's ridiculous," said Kate. "Look, just because I express some concerns about the product doesn't mean I'm a saboteur."

"We thought maybe it got out through the ad agency," I tried to explain.

"I haven't even talked to the agency," roared Kate. "The name FlyingFox has never passed my lips with those people."

Cub and I studied the pattern on our plates carefully and said nothing.

"Come on," she continued, irked. "I know you think I'm not committed to this team, and you're right. I'm not committed the way you are. But let's not start getting clannish. Just because I'm not a team member exactly as you'd like me to be doesn't mean I'm an enemy."

"You're right, Kate," I said. "It's just that MarTech is breathing down our necks and we're very concerned they don't get the jump on us. Now, can we just forget about it?"

Kate considered. "Sure. But just remember that there are all kinds of team players. I may not be a true Fox, but I believe that I'm a team player. Okay?"

I wasn't entirely convinced. This protest might have been nothing but a performance on Kate's part, but I couldn't think of any good reason for her to leak information.

The talk turned to focus groups, marketing plans, and the FlyingFox launch. Kate still had not thought through what needed to be done, had not considered whether to use her existing agencies or retain new ones, and was far from doing any detailed work.

"It's too early for all that, Ron. Anything I work up now probably would be useless by the time we go to market."

"Maybe, but I'm thinking about Judgment Day. Jasper has told me the steering committee will be interested in marketing plans and sales programs. We need to give them some specifics."

"There's no point in doing the work twice. Why should I invest a lot of time in developing all that stuff for this presentation when I know it will change in the long run? It's not efficient."

"Do you mean, why invest all that effort when there's still a possibility the project will be cancelled?"

Kate shrugged. "You could put it that way. Is that unreasonable? I'm telling you that you'll get the best effort out of me and my people after Judgment Day, when we're closer to launch and FlyingFox is in a more final form."

"I would feel more comfortable if we had some concepts and ideas in development," I said, "and I think the steering committee would, too."

Kate looked at me obstinately. "I'm not doing anything on FlyingFox until after it gets approved. I think that's the best way to do it. If you don't like that, get rid of me."

I didn't know what to say to her. "Kate, I want you on the team. I respect your talent. I want your contribution."

"Then relax," she said. "Have another glass of water."

36. *The Bag Factor.*

After lunch, Cub and I bade farewell to Kate and roared off in Cub's Mercedes.

"Don't worry about her," said Cub.

"No?"

"She's good; she'll come through. I've seen her do it plenty of times."

I had not worked with Kate on a launch of this kind. Cub's opinion reassured me.

"Besides, she was mad that we had accused her of being the source of the leak."

"Rightfully so. We could have handled that a little more delicately."

Our destination was the annual congregation and trade

show of the International Office Technology Systems Forum (IOTSF), which attracts all the heavyweights in our industry, both suppliers and customers. Cub and I wanted to do some snooping around, see who was up to what and what was up to who.

As we entered the municipal arena our first impression was that we had entered MarTech Mall. It seemed that everyone was carrying a shiny black and gold plastic shopping bag with MARTECH! emblazoned on both sides. This was a severe blow to our corporate egos. We had long considered IOTSF to be FCI's show. For years, FCI bought the largest booth, which generally remained packed from the ten o'clock opening until the cleaners arrived twelve hours later. We kept more than one hotel busy with seminars, demo rooms, and hospitality suites.

Two years ago, however, during the Purge, allocations for "nonadvertising promotional activities" had been reduced. Our show expenditures dropped, we lost our favored position with the organizers, and then it all disintegrated into bickering.

If superficial appearances are a measure of anything, and of course they are, the IOTSF visitor this year would have to assume that FCI had dropped off the map and that MarTech had taken our place. All shopping bags seemed to lead to the MarTech booth, a slick new structure that sat smugly on a substantial chunk of prime trade-show real estate just inside the front entrance. It was bustling with people. Standing room only at the multimedia presentation. Salespeople in earnest conversation with customers within glass-walled conference rooms. Smiling MarTech martinets handing out shopping bags and giveaway goodies to passersby.

Cub and I felt like aliens on our own turf. It spooked us both. I thought, FCI has been supplanted. FlyingFox can be the best product in the world and no one will notice, or care if they do. We might as well give up on it.

"Hey, Red!"

I was watching a MarTech video that was blah-blahing about "open systems compatibility" and "flexibility" and "networking options" when I heard the voice at my elbow.

"Red! Where's the old Fick this year?!"

I knew who the voice had to belong to, because only one person had ever called me Red, much to my annoyance. I checked the name badge to be sure: Donnell Ware, MarTech Global Accounts Manager.

"Donnell," I said and shook his hand. "I didn't know you were with MarTech." Donnell and I had worked together, pre-FCI, for about three years at a now-defunct company.

Donnell smiled. "Oh yeah. They dragged me away from my old job. They made me just too good an offer. Uprooted the family and everything."

Knowing Donnell, it was just as likely that he had been bounced from his old job or sleazed his way into MarTech. It didn't matter. MarTech was hiring, and knowing Donnell's skills, they weren't being terribly discriminating. Whatever my opinion of him, Donnell looked fit and prosperous. He, like all the MarTech people, was dressed in a specially tailored jacket with MARTECH! running down the sleeves.

"Congratulations!" I tried to sound positive, and not in the least bit threatened.

"FCI decided it couldn't compete with us, so you took your ball and went home this year, huh?" Donnell was not going to give up on FCI's absence.

"We made a strategic decision not to take part in the show this year. We're putting more resources into the SESG show, but don't tell anyone." This was more or less true, but it was a decision I had not agreed with.

Donnell made a face. "The SESG show is a dog. No one goes to that show any more. It's dead."

"We don't feel that way," I said, feeling exactly that way.

Someone called to Donnell from across the booth. "Donnell, can you help us over here for a minute?"

"Be right there!" replied Donnell. He lowered his voice and leaned closer to me.

"Are you planning to introduce this new system I've been hearing about at the SESG show?"

"Which new system is that?"

"This one that Shark Design is involved in. Voice response. Some new recyclable composite material."

He knew about the material already! "I don't know what you're talking about."

"Come on, Ron, we don't have a competitive product. Don't worry."

140

"That's not what I hear," I said.

"Well, even if we did, we don't want to completely take over the market, you know. We need a little competition from a nice sedate company like the Fick."

"Where did you hear this rumor?"

"It's all over the show. Everybody knows you're trying to speed up your development process." He lowered his voice even further. "And everyone knows you're constipated in the R&D department."

"Oh, really." I bristled despite my attempts to appear unconcerned.

"But getting Shark involved sounds like a smart idea. Get some fresh blood in there."

I said nothing.

Donnell smiled and changed the subject. "Hey, take a look at some of the futures stuff we're showing in there." Donnell pointed to a smoked-glass enclosure marked MARTECH TOMORROW. "Exciting stuff!"

Donnell shook my hand again and handed me his card. "Keep in touch, Ron." In a gesture of politeness to the enemy, I gave him one of my cards as well. Donnell stared at it and tapped it against the back of his thumb.

"Might give you a call one of these days."

"What about?"

"Oh . . ."

"Donnell!" the voice called again.

"Got to dash," he said, tucking my card in his pocket. He rushed off to attend to his customer and I wandered through the Tomorrow section, wondering why Donnell would want to talk to anyone from "old" FCI?

Cub and I spent the entire afternoon at the show and came away with bundles of literature, which Cub shoved into a MarTech bag.

"Cub, you're a disgrace to the Fickie clan. You're a walking advertisement for the competition."

Cub shrugged. "You've got to walk in the enemy's shoes to understand what they're all about, Ron."

"That doesn't mean you have to carry their bag."

"Look at it this way, Ron," he said. "This is a nice bag.

141

Probably cost them a buck apiece. And they just wasted it on me. I'm helping reduce their bottom line."

The bag ended up pinned to the wall of the Lair, along with the *Fortune* cover photo of MarTech CEO J. Sanford Picker. When things were slow (which was seldom), we amused ourselves by throwing darts at them.

37. *Fox Talk.*

To: Ron
From: Martha

How's it going, Ron? Haven't heard from you in a while. That probably means you're doing okay. Just checking in.

To: Martha
From: Ron

Thanks for your note. We're doing well, after weathering some crises. But now that you bring it up, any thoughts on how best to really evaluate our performance? Can there be one set of performance criteria for judging all team members' performance? Or do you judge your people on each person's individual goals?

And how about the team's progress, as a whole? The ultimate criterion is FlyingFox, of course, its success in the marketplace. The results. But we can't use that as an interim measurement. What do you suggest?

To: Ron
From: Martha

I think you have to judge all team members, first of all, against the ground rules. You know, attendance at meetings, participation, working together, etc. But the more important evaluation is based on each person's performance in comparison to the responsibilities you established with each one at the beginning. (You did do that, didn't you?)

And, sure, there are plenty of ways to evaluate how the team is doing as a whole. You probably discussed them in your training course. E.g.:

Is everybody contributing?

Are you getting a balance between the amount of time you
spend on people and process issues (how efficient/effective
are we?) and task issues (how is the product/project itself
progressing?)?

Is *your* role as leader changing at all? Are you pushing less and
enjoying it more?

Has anybody left the team? How and why?

Are the team members getting more or less support from their
functional managers?

Are there any promising flickers of enthusiasm, excitement,
unexpected ideas, unwarranted heroism?

Are you finding opportunities to praise and reward people? And
do they respond?

What do the team members think? Do they feel that the team is
making progress?

It's simple, Ronnie!

FOXFILE ENTRY:

• The team has reached a kind of self-knowledge that allows us to
spend less time on internal issues and more time on the tasks at hand.
More time solving problems, less time assigning blame.

That doesn't mean that we are all completely satisfied with each other
or our procedures. But we do understand each other and our
boundaries better. We're beyond storming. We're well into our
"norming" phase—and on the brink of performing.

38. *Keeper of the Network.*

Things hummed along quietly for the next few weeks. The
product team had successfully created a prototype with an appealing FungiFlex housing. My budgets and forecasts were under control. Kate and Andrea were organizing a post–Judgment
Day focus group, in anticipation of receiving approval. Phyllis,
who had done all the purchasing work for our videoconferencing system and some computer hardware for the Lair, had developed an amateur's keen interest in computer systems and
information technology.

We had one week to go before Judgment Day. I was in the
Lair that Monday morning, a sharply focused early September

day, working with Andrea (and still reveling in a 3–2 win for the Tibias, during which I had not once screamed from the sidelines). Andrea was coordinating the presentation itself, which was to take place over the following weekend at The Woods, a sprawling conference center at the edge of a state forest, about two hours away. She had created a detailed time-line, tacking up a series of flipchart pages that now encircled the room. At each critical milestone, she had written a brief list of the tasks involved and who was responsible for each. We were reviewing it together, making some adjustments here and there, when the phone rang.

"Ron, this is Jocelyn Veens from MIS." Management Information Systems. She sounded angry.

"Yes, Jocelyn?"

"Listen, I've just been talking with a computer systems person from some company called Shark Design?"

"Yes."

"I don't know how he got my name, or why he's calling me directly, but he was making some assumptions about our network that disturbed me, and I'd like to discuss them with you."

"All right." I had no idea what this was about.

"It seems that this design firm has linked in directly with our engineering people. They can share files and various types of company information?"

"Yes. I'm not fully aware of the technical details, but—"

"Why was MIS not consulted on this?" Jocelyn was not pleased.

Why hadn't we consulted them? I remembered that I had thought about meeting with them, and then, oh yes, Shark took on the responsibility of investigating the linkup. "I'd have to talk with my engineering people," I said, "but it was a de-partmental matter that didn't involve the central data resource and our subcontractor had experience in that area, so—"

"Ron, it's my responsibility to maintain a coherent infor-mation technology strategy for the entire company. I know you're one of the New World teams. I know you're under pres-sure, and I know you've gotten a mandate to throw your weight around a bit."

I couldn't recall ever receiving such a mandate. "I wouldn't say that."

"But, Ron," she continued, "we can't have every team running off and buying their own systems and hooking up with outside suppliers willy-nilly."

"I understand that, but what we found was that we didn't have the systems in place to connect the people we needed to get connected."

"That may be so, but this is precisely the kind of ad hoc effort we're trying to discourage. I know you're thinking of what's good for your FlyingFox team. But you also have to think in terms of the *entire* team, which is, in effect, the company."

"Yes." There are so many loyalties to be attended to when you work in a large company. Yourself. Your manager. Your work group. Your team. Your discipline. Your colleagues. The people you manage. The customer. The company. The industry. Your family. The country. I felt that I had little loyalty left to devote to my company's computer network.

"Plus," said Jocelyn, "there are some serious security issues to deal with here. I don't know what kind of arrangement you have with these Shark people, but you're essentially sharing proprietary information with them. Not only that, the simple fact that you've established a link with them makes us more vulnerable. It's not inconceivable that they could hack into our corporate systems databases and get access to highly confidential sales and marketing information. Payroll. Personnel. Everything."

"Is that possible?"

"Yes, and I think it should be obvious that if the information were to get into the wrong hands . . ."

I thought about the Shark rumors and wondered if our leak was an electronic one. "What do we need to do?"

"In addition," continued Jocelyn, "my E-mail system administrator tells me that the system is being used for a good deal of personal correspondence."

"How do you know that?"

"She read some of the messages."

"You mean you can go into private E-mailboxes and read personal mail?"

"Well, we discovered these personal messages when we were cleaning up the hard drive. When you delete a message on your PC, it actually is stored in memory, although it leaves your system. We have to clean it out periodically or we'd be overwhelmed with junk."

"But isn't that an invasion of privacy?"

"The network is a corporate asset, Ron. It belongs to FCI. Employees use it as a business tool, just like any other tool they're issued in order to get their jobs done. Suppose some guy in the tool room started building birdhouses on the corporate lathes."

"Happens all the time."

Jocelyn did not laugh. "Perhaps so, but it's a little more serious when it comes to the FCI computer network. People are running businesses, selling used cars, posting personal messages, you name it. We have to try to control it, and that means reading mail."

"Okay, but back to the topic at hand, we've got two issues here," I said. "As far as the link with Shark goes, I'm not the right person to deal with it, and I'll have to get back to you. And this business about personal use. I'd like to hear some other opinions on that one."

"I'm very uncomfortable with this Shark relationship. I think FCI is at risk, so if I don't get satisfactory information by tomorrow I'll have to take action."

"Such as?"

"I may have to temporarily break the connection."

"Jocelyn, that link to Shark is a vital one to our team. Maybe there are a few personal notes flowing through the system, but I'm sure the traffic is mostly engineering drawings and design documents. I cannot allow that connection to be interrupted."

Jocelyn backed off slightly. "At the very least, we have to check out the security procedures."

After she hung up, I got angry.

To: Jasper
From: Ron

What authority does MIS have over our team's computing systems? Jocelyn is bent out of shape because we've established a link with Shark and she's even threatened to break it. Clearly, the team structure is not to her liking. She wants centralization. You told us we would have substantial autonomy.

How do we avoid a showdown on this? I don't want to spend this week wrangling with MIS when I should be polishing the presentation to the steering committee.

To: Ron
From: Jasper

Your team's behavior has an impact on everyone else in the organization. A team cannot function without support from the entire organization. Jocelyn is faced with a difficult challenge: she has to redesign a computer network with roots in the Old World so that it serves the flatter, team-based New World. There's a lot of money and effort represented in all the hardware and software we use. I don't think she's deliberately trying to thwart you. She's just trying to do her job.

However, her threat to cut the connection was out of line. Please try to negotiate/cooperate with her. If you need me to get involved let me know.

To: Team FF
From: Ron
Re: Information Technology

I have been informed that the E-mail system is considered a corporate asset, paid for and administered by FCI. That means:

1. It is not a suitable medium for confidential information. Nor should it be used for personal communications.

2. We should consider the possibility that rumors and sensitive information about FlyingFox are being leaked through the network.

Jocelyn Veens, the MIS director, is concerned about security, about our outside partners getting into the corporate sales and marketing databases. Could Nick or Wes please be in contact with her *today*. Please communicate with each other and let me know who is the best person to handle this.

To: Ron
From: Hartmut

My computer people inform me that Shark has no way to tap into FCI's corporate information. We had enough trouble sharing design files. Besides, we take our relationship with FCI very seriously. We would not do anything to jeopardize it.

To: Ron
From: Wesley

I'll talk with Jocelyn. We speak the same language. I'm sure we can work this out.

To: Ron
From: Andrea

How does Jocelyn know there are personal communications going over the network? She obviously is opening private mail. Is that legal? Is it moral? Did you challenge her on it?

By the way, she's probably talking about Keith and me. We've exchanged a few personal messages, but I really don't think we're abusing the system. Is the mailroom manager authorized to open personal letters?

To: Ron
From: Cub

Hey, while you're at it, how about talking to Jocelyn about laptops for the sales force. We want them !!!!!

To: Andrea
From: Ron

Jocelyn did not say who the personal messages were from or to and I didn't ask. It's none of my business, and none of hers. Just keep in mind that what you think is private may not be.

To: Ron
From: Wesley

Jocelyn is calmed down. No real threat to system. She just wants to be kept informed from now on.

To: Ron
From: Carlos

Could you meet me for a drink tonight? Something important to discuss with you.

FOXFILE ENTRY:

• Autonomy and empowerment are relative terms. As independent and self-sufficient as our team may be, we still are part of the larger organization. We get into trouble when we think of ourselves as autonomous. We may administer our own behavior, but there is still a higher authority to whom we must answer. And I do mean authority.

39. *Our First Defection.*

That evening at six-thirty, rather than wending my pleasant way home to my scrappy and unpredictable home team (whom I had seen less of than I liked since the inauguration of FlyingFox), I was waiting for Carlos to join me at a local restaurant. I toyed with the breadsticks and tried to guess what he had to say. Something about FungiFlex? About Hartmut? Maybe he had some personal problem. I had come to expect crisis from Carlos, or at least the sense of crisis.

Carlos hustled in the door and surveyed the tables, repositioning his heavy gold ID bracelet with a chronic wiggle of his right wrist as he searched for me. I waved at him and he reflexively checked the other diners in the restaurant, then hurried over to the table and slipped into the chair.

"Thanks for coming, Ron. I wanted to tell you this firsthand, before anyone else gets wind of it."

"What's up, Carlos?" He was distracted and tense. "Is everything all right?"

Carlos dropped his guard, realizing that I was going to be sympathetic.

"Yes, everything is fine. I just have some news that will affect you." Carlos clasped his hands, scrunched forward in his chair, and looked at the placemat. "I'm leaving FCI."

"When?"

"Two weeks. I haven't told anybody. Not even Jasper. But I thought you should know before the Woods presentation. I know how much you care about FlyingFox. I didn't want to go through the presentation and then disappear on you."

"I appreciate that." If we had been developing just another project in just the same old way, Carlos probably would not have taken the trouble to warn me about his departure. There was, in an odd sense, a loyalty to the team in his manner of leaving it. He didn't want to hurt our chances. "Where are you going?" I asked.

Carlos brightened. "I've been offered a spectacular opportunity. I can't tell you the name of the company, but they are very progressive and they want me to develop a whole new manufacturing organization in Europe. It means designing and opening two new facilities, and getting six others into shape. It's a lot of responsibility and they're ready to sink substantial resources into the work."

"It's not MarTech, is it?"

Carlos laughed. "No, no, no. That would *really* be a defection."

"But did you interview with them?"

"Yes, I did. That's, in fact, why I couldn't come to your party. I was out there over that weekend."

"Did you discuss FlyingFox with them?"

Carlos bristled. "No, not at all. That would be unethical."

It also would be a simple explanation for our leaks.

"Congratulations then."

"Yes, two of the plants will be in Eastern Europe, so it's going to be a tremendous challenge."

"But couldn't you have done the same thing with FCI? We have manufacturing operations in Europe."

"Sure. But it's not just Europe that attracts me. I feel undervalued at FCI. Here I come in and make North River a showplace plant, one of the most productive in our industry, and I get absolutely no credit. I mean, my position has not changed at all. I've gotten no promotion. I haven't been asked to develop any new plants, or even share what we've done with the rest of the organization. I sometimes think that it's discrimination, that they think 'Oh, that Mexican guy, what can he teach us?' And I'm not even Mexican."

"I doubt that, Carlos," I said.

"Case in point is that FanFare component I told you about at our first meeting. Did you ever have a chance to look into that?"

"Yes," I said uncomfortably. "The word I got was that the FanFare people were worried about working with you."

"With me?" erupted Carlos. He scoffed. "That's ridiculous. I bent over backward for them. They had never received such a detailed proposal. They probably couldn't even see how good it was."

"I'm just reporting what I learned. The word they used was *peevish*."

"*Peevish?* They called me peevish? There's a perfect example of why I'm leaving. All the personal politics. I believe that business is about results, not about who you like to work with."

"I agree, Carlos. Now, who's going to take over for you with FlyingFox?"

Carlos waved his hand as if this were a matter of no significance. "Nelson can do everything I can do. He's been the point man for FlyingFox so far. Besides, all the information is in the system. All of the pilot runs, test results and so forth, I mean *all* the information that has anything to do with manufacturing FlyingFox, is in one place on the computer. I'm not taking any information with me in my head that you're going to need. It's all there. I believe in corporate memory."

"But, certainly, there has to be some seat-of-the-pants stuff, some hunches and feelings that are important."

Carlos shook his head violently. "No, no, no. That's what I mean by corporate memory. What we've done at North River is ensure that no one person can hold the keys to the success of any enterprise."

"What do you mean?"

"Have you ever heard of the black arts?"

"No."

"The black arts are the manufacturing knowledge that traditionally doesn't get written down anywhere. It isn't on the plans of the machine tools, it's not in the computer data. But it's a lot of information you have to have to run a plant and build any given product properly. And it's stored in people's heads."

"Give me an example."

"Oh, that you have to run a milling machine a little slower than spec, or remove a sixteenth of an inch more material than it shows on the plan. Or that you get bad product from some machine when the humidity is over ninety percent. There are a million things like that that no one tells anybody else—for a bunch of different reasons—but without them your factory won't run right. Or, I should say, that's the way it used to be."

"North River isn't that way?"

"No. We don't believe in the black arts. I got burned badly as a young man when I was running my first plant."

"How?"

"We were manufacturing a complicated component in our U.S. plant, and needed to increase capacity. I was the number two guy at the U.S. plant then. I'd only been on the job for about a year. But I had done well, so management decided that it was time to start manufacturing overseas and that I should oversee the startup. They figured it was simple—I just had to take the plans over, get them started, and then come home."

Carlos ran his fingers through his hair, and nervously wriggled his ID bracelet. "It was a disaster. They tooled up, started the run. And they couldn't make the component. They couldn't do it!"

Carlos laughed, but with an edge of pain at the memory.

"I was over there for months trying to figure out the problem. My arrogant first assumption was that they were too stupid to read the plans. But, no, that wasn't the problem. They were doing everything right, it was the plans and the drawings that were a little bit off. The information they needed was in people's memories back home, not in corporate memory."

I pictured a young Carlos, wanting to do well on his first big assignment, and trying to make sense of a new plant out of control.

"What did you do?"

"I came back home and pried the information out of all the guys on the line. I went back and we finally got things going. But I vowed I would never allow that to happen to me again. And that's why I've spent so much time creating a plant at North River that has a memory."

"How?"

"We use our information technology to store and utilize people's best ideas. It's automation of knowledge, if you see what I mean. It's using information that we gather from the process, and then feeding it back into the process to inform and guide how we do things. Ever read *In the Age of the Smart Machine?*"

It was on my bookshelf, waiting to be read. "No, not yet."

"The author talks about *informating*. Manufacturing automation used to be about automating. About using computers to control machines. Well, informating is about gathering information about quality, about yield rates, cycle times and all that, and using it to improve your manufacturing process—cycling it back into the process. Informating is about really *using* your information, not just collecting it. That's what I've done at North River. And that's why my leaving really will not affect your ability to get FlyingFox off the ground."

I began to see Carlos in a new light, and felt for the first time that we would be losing a real asset. I hadn't been able to understand his message, partially because it kept getting obscured by his irascible temperament, partially because I hadn't listened carefully enough. I wondered if we could have kept him if I had listened better.

"Carlos, I don't think anyone at FCI understands that's what you've been doing at North River."

"Some people do. Jocelyn Veens does."

"But the rest of us hear you say that you've created a special plant, better than any other in the industry. We don't understand why, so it sounds like boasting. Don't you think you could use FlyingFox to help change the perception of North River at FCI?"

"Maybe. But I've made up my mind, Ron. I'm leaving."

"Just tell me what you think our chances are with FlyingFox, now that you can speak freely."

Carlos leaned forward, his eyes sparkling. "Are you kidding? You have a fabulous product on your hands. I have nothing but respect for Shark Design, no matter how *peevish* Hartmut is. FungiFlex is a good material. I am impressed by the commitment you've gotten from all your people. I think you're going to give the company a big boot forward!"

I was not expecting praise from Carlos.

"Stay then. Help us out."

Carlos waved his head from side to side, eyes still twinkling. "Then again, you could bomb. What would happen to me then?"

- There is some regret when a team member leaves, whatever the working relationship has been. But comings and goings are simply a part of the corporate life. The team is a necessarily fluid thing. If the team isn't strong enough to withstand a change of personnel, it isn't strong enough to survive.

40. *The Fox Barks.*

Judgment Saturday was upon us. By ten o'clock Friday morning we were assembled for rehearsal. Wesley, Nick, Andrea, Cub, Phyllis, Nelson, and me. Kate was late. Keith and Hartmut were due to arrive at about noon. Zanoski had promised to stop in after lunch.

Andrea had done a thorough job of organizing our presentation materials, and we began by reviewing them—a series of large boards that contained the key areas we would cover: Team members; program objectives; FlyingFox features and benefits. Competitive product comparisons. Program costs. Sales forecasts and breakeven. Manufacturing schedule. Key marketing and promotional activities, including public relations. Andrea and I had developed this last, by default, since Kate had so steadfastly refused to do any work before Judgment Day.

The *pièce de résistance* was to be our reveal (airbreather term for unveiling) of the latest FlyingFox prototype. It had arrived at rehearsal in a large cardboard box, but Nick and Wesley had refused to show it to any of us because it was awaiting the latest version of its outer skin, fashioned in FungiFlex, which was coming from Shark with Hartmut and Keith.

We worked our way through our parts, each taking his or her turn, and receiving comments and feedback as we went along. By noon, we felt reasonably confident that we had a solid presentation and that nothing substantial was missing. Whether or not the steering committee would view FlyingFox as positively as we did was an imponderable.

It was time to reveal the prototype—which, in fact, was a working model built with about 7 percent production (as opposed to hand-built) parts—but Hartmut and Keith had not yet arrived, and Nick begged us to wait for them.

"You'll see only the guts of the machine and the old housing," he said. "You'll hate it."

We decided to eat lunch, and give them another hour. By

quarter past one they still had not arrived. Andrea called the Shark office and was told that Hartmut and Keith were en route and should be arriving at any moment. We decided to go ahead. Just as Wesley and Nick were placing the box at the center of the conference table, Zanoski slipped into the room. With him was Kate. By entering with Zanoski—Who knows how she orchestrated it?—she made it seem that she and Dr. Z were part of some ruling body that had come to review our work and pass judgment. I knew that we could not show the prototype in its crude state to these two.

"Ah, you're about to review the prototype!" said Zanoski, with enthusiasm. "I am just in time."

"Yes," echoed Kate. "Finally we can get our hands on the real thing and see if it's going to fly or not." She smiled at Zanoski knowingly and positioned herself next to him at the table, placing her large white handbag at her side and then lifting her chin as if to say, "We are ready."

I could feel the Foxes closing ranks against her. Kate was doing another one of her flip-flops. At our recent lunch together, I had left with the impression that she was part of the team. Now here she was, masquerading as a Zanoski crony and management insider. Zanoski sensed the tension in the room and immediately understood its source. He leaned forward.

"Ron, I am here to help in any way I can. You know that the decision to go forward with FlyingFox is entirely to be made by the steering committee."

This distanced Zanoski from Kate slightly, and everyone relaxed a little. She was oblivious.

"But this Fox better be good." She used her most grating tone, trying to make a joke, and failing. "You've got some stiff competition from the other New World projects. I've seen three of them so far and it's going to be a tough decision. Even Dick's Ficus thing isn't as pathetic as I thought it might be."

I wanted to give the team reason not to be intimidated by Kate's attitude and make it clear to her that she was either part of the team or she wasn't. I also wanted to buy a little time for Hartmut and Keith to arrive.

"Kate, we've been waiting to review the prototype until the Shark people get here. Perhaps while we're waiting, we could talk about promotional and advertising plans."

"I told you Ron, it's premature to talk about advertising and promotions yet. I thought we agreed to wait until after Judgment Day."

"Yes. But Andrea and I have developed a preliminary plan. And we'd like to get your reactions, at the very least."

Zanoski shot a curious look at Kate. "I should think you would be developing marketing plans right along with the product," he said. "Isn't that the whole idea behind New World teams? That we coordinate the functions, so that marketing can have a strong voice in product development? We may not like it, but it must be good for us." He made a small, sour face that was both self-effacing and funny.

Kate squirmed a little, but countered strongly. "Listen, it's futile to develop any plans before the product is ready."

"I know that's how you feel," I said and pushed no further. Kate glared at me. I had dared to rebuke her, however mildly, in front of Zanoski. After an awkward pause, we returned our attention to the cardboard box and I began to say something about how we were still working on the housing when I heard the back doors open.

We heard a bark, a foxlike yipping. It was Keith doing an imitation of a FlyingFox. Hartmut, beside him, was wearing the FlyingFox toy, fashioned as a hat. He shook his head furiously, and the fox wagged its tail.

"Do not open that box!" commanded Hartmut.

I looked at Zanoski, not knowing how he would react to these antics. There was a vague smile on his face. Hartmut and Keith sauntered to the table and Hartmut held out his hand to Zanoski.

"Dr. Zanoski, I am honored to meet you."

While Dr. Z and Hartmut exchanged greetings, Keith snatched the box away without a word and wagged his head to Nick and Wesley to join him, and the three of them dashed to the back of the room to assemble FlyingFox.

"I'm sorry to be late," said Hartmut, "but we were unavoidably delayed."

He glanced toward the back of the room, nodded at the boys, and called, "Good morning, FlyingFox!"

We heard a woman's voice reply, "Good morning!"

All heads turned. There was no woman at the back of the room. It was FlyingFox talking.

Keith, Nick, and Wesley proudly marched to the table carrying the prototype. I must confess that after all those months of looking at crude models and skinless constructions, this was the first one that lifted my spirits. They set FlyingFox at the center of the table and we all gazed at it. It *looked* like a delightful product. Modern and rounded, but not me-too in shape. There were simple, elegant controls. A soothing, deep forest green color. And perhaps most intriguing of all, the material. FungiFlex felt resilient to the touch but not squishy. The machine looked solid and strong, yet when you picked it up, it was surprisingly light. Kate ran her hand across the Fox surface, then looked directly at Zanoski.

"The material is *wonderful!* It's so different. It's a breakthrough. It will be a huge customer selling point."

Zanoski didn't look at her. "Yes," he said, deep in thought, "perhaps." He was studying the machine, finger to his lips. He turned to Nick. "May we have a full demo?"

Wesley, Nick, Hartmut, and Nelson (who had begun to come out of his Carlos-induced shell and chimed in enthusiastically about manufacturing issues) spent the next two hours demonstrating all the functions and explaining the various features of the machine. By the time we finished, it was approaching four o'clock. It had been a grueling session, as we poked and prodded, discussing every detail of our creation. Everybody had joined in, with the exception of Kate, who, after her first outburst of enthusiasm, sat silently, arms crossed, listening. Dr. Z had provided some insightful comments about the design and about manufacturing and marketing issues. When Hartmut praised the characteristics of the F-Flex material, Dr. Z could not hide his delight. He lit up like a child.

"It's good, isn't it? You really find it workable?"

"Yes," said Hartmut, "and I would like to recommend it to some other clients."

Zanoski puckered his lips. "Ah, well, it really isn't ready. It needs . . ."

He stopped.

"It needs?" prodded Hartmut.

"Perhaps you're right. Yes, perhaps we could collaborate.

We could provide the material and you could experiment with it."

"Let's talk further."

We concluded the session with a sense that despite the problems to be resolved, we were about where we should be in the development process. But, as we were wrapping up, Kate's judgmental silence intensified. She became actively quiet.

"You haven't said much, Kate. What do you think?" I forced myself to ask.

Once again, all eyes were on her. This, perhaps, was her real and overriding desire—to keep attention focused on her, rather than make any specific plays for power or approbation. She simply liked being the center of things.

"I reserve judgment," she said.

"Come on. We want your reactions and feedback."

"Okay, I think it's going to have problems in overseas markets."

"Why?"

"The voice response is a gimmick. Europeans won't like that." She said it as if it were a fact, rather than an opinion.

"What do you think, Hartmut?" I asked.

Hartmut wagged his head side to side. "Perhaps. Perhaps two years ago that would have been true. I think maybe now the market is ready."

"Besides," Phyllis boldly interjected, "you can turn it off. You don't have to use it."

"The customer still has to pay for it," said Kate. "It'll be perceived as an unnecessary cost."

"But we don't plan to roll it out in Europe until after we see how it plays in the U.S." Nick protested.

"Oh, really? Who made that decision?" This was encroaching on her turf.

"Well, that's what we had discussed," Nick said, retreating.

"I believe we talked in general about launch plans at one of the staff meetings you couldn't attend," I said.

"No one talked to me about that."

"It was in the meeting minutes."

"I never saw it," said Kate.

"I suggest we table the issue until our next meeting," I said to Kate, wanting to keep this controversy from scuttling the presentation.

"Sure," she said, with a show of reasonableness. "But there is one other thing I'd like to bring up, which might have a bearing on our presentation."

Kate hauled a stack of computer printouts from her briefcase and plunked them on the table. "This is some rather interesting marketing research that I just had completed."

She removed a thin report from her briefcase and flipped to the first page. Everyone in the room stared at her. It was like watching an attorney introducing a new witness at the very end of a trial. What was she doing? Whatever this research might be, it, in conjunction with her weird behavior and obstreperous comments during this meeting, was alienating her from the other team members.

"It's an analysis of the buying patterns of the Fortune 1000 companies for similar equipment retailing at the price points we're considering for FlyingFox."

I checked my watch. It was time to get rolling for The Woods.

"How will this help us with our presentation tomorrow, Kate?" I asked.

"It gives us a better understanding of our market, which, I might add, is shrinking fast. What it shows is that Fox will be flying right into a saturated market where spending is down."

"But that doesn't mean that a new product couldn't make a substantial impact," Andrea argued. "FlyingFox is new. It could revitalize the market."

"Anything's possible," said Kate. No one in the group seemed very interested in her research. Zanoski was already tapping his fingers against his thigh, obviously eager to get away.

"But here's what's most interesting," she continued more urgently, flipping to the next page.

"Kate," I cut her off. "We need to get moving to The Woods. We've really completed our agenda for today. I'd be happy to discuss this information further with you. But I think we should adjourn."

The team looked at me gratefully. "Okay." Kate beamed at everyone. "Just trying to make a contribution. Like you keep telling me to. Share the information." She slapped the report shut. "But here it is. It's available if anybody's interested. I'll bring it along with me."

Kate's swings of mood and shifting tactics had become increasingly unpredictable. I had to find a way to handle her more successfully.

"Fine," I said lamely. "Thank you."

The meeting adjourned, but there was an uneasiness about the group as we gathered our belongings and headed for the parking lot. Was that Kate's intention? Just to keep us off balance? Dr. Zanoski took me aside in the hallway.

"Ron. I just want to wish you luck at tomorrow's presentation. I think FlyingFox has great promise."

"Thank you, Doctor. You didn't catch any serious problems we've overlooked?"

"I expressed all my concerns during the meeting." His eyes dropped. "I further want to say that I think FlyingFox is a good choice for the debut of FungiFlex. I am grateful for the collaboration."

Dr. Z. was thanking *me* for using his new material.

I chuckled. "Thanks for letting Nick continue with the project."

Zanoski nodded. "Good." And then he hurried away.

When I set out on the New World team, I expected the rewards to take the form of recognition from bosses and maybe money or position. None of those things, of course, would be unappreciated should they materialize. However, I had not thought about this kind of recognition and reward: from my peers and colleagues. It was especially welcome.

I drove. Hartmut joined me in the front seat, Andrea and Keith sat together in the back. We all were tired after the long rehearsal.

Hartmut was talking to me. "Sorry we were late, Ron."

I had forgotten they were late. "Flight delayed?"

Hartmut said, with no trace of emotion, "We had a little glitch."

"Oh?"

"Nothing serious. We fixed it. But we had to catch a later plane."

"What kind of glitch?"

"A little software bug. A little error in the code, we think. It affected the voice response system."

"But you solved it?" I didn't even know the right questions to ask about software bugs.

"Don't worry."

He seemed confident and so I put the problem out of my mind. I looked in the rear-view mirror. Both Andrea and Keith had fallen asleep, his arm draped along the back of the seat behind her, her head lolling toward his shoulder.

41. *Arriving at Yes.*

We completed our presentation to the steering committee at two-thirty on the dot that Saturday afternoon. We had presented well, and the FlyingFox prototype had made a strong impression on the committee members. If I had to bet, based on the tone of the steering committee's questions, I would guess they were inclined to give us approval. We would not know for sure until Sunday, but we decided to celebrate that night anyway. Besides, Hartmut and Keith were due to fly home Sunday morning, and we wanted to share the evening with them. In fact, it was Hartmut, a lover of food and wine, who made the suggestion that the entire team go out for dinner, booked a private room in the main restaurant at The Woods, and conferred with the chef.

The weather was kind to us. It was a spectacular fall day, and so that afternoon we had taken advantage of The Woods' recreational facilities. I played nine holes of golf with Cub and Phyllis, and she proved to be a stubborn competitor, beating us both by two strokes. Wesley, Nelson, Martha, and Kate played doubles on the clay courts. Andrea and Keith went rollerblading on a network of paved trails that meandered deep into the pine woods surrounding the resort. Nick and Hartmut, an unlikely pair, had gone off running together, Hartmut wearing a pair of old tennis shoes, Nick in a pair of cross trainers of the latest multicolored, space-age material.

By the time we gathered for dinner, everyone was relaxed and in good spirits. An appetizer appeared just after we sat down—a tiny puff pastry in the shape of a fox, stuffed with some sort of foxy-reddish filling. It was accompanied by champagne. Hartmut raised his glass.

"To Team FlyingFox!" he said.

We drank. The champagne was exceptional. I felt a twinge of uneasiness. Who was going to pay for all this? Hartmut or me? Either way, I figured that FlyingFox would be paying in the end, and wondered if we were being a bit extravagant for a New World team that had no revenue yet and wasn't even officially funded. Then I decided that after months of hard work, we deserved a reward.

I raised my glass to everyone assembled. "I just want to . . ." I wasn't sure what I wanted to say although the words "thank you" were, in fact, on the tip of my tongue.

"I was going to say thank you," I began. "But to say thank you implies that you've done what you've done to please *me*. For my approval and thanks. And, believe me, I am not so naive as to imagine that that had anything to do with it. That's the way it should be, because the New World is not about bosses and ass-kissing, and hierarchy and job titles." I paused, and shook my head in mock regret. "No, those were the good old days. But they're gone." Laughter.

"Today, we are—or trying to be, anyway—simply a group of people with diverse skills and attitudes, working together to get a specific job done. We still have our personal agendas. We still have our conflicts. But no one ever said that working as a team means that we have to be in harmony all the time. Or even very much of the time. What it does mean is that we're able to balance our personal goals with our team responsibilities. That we're able to work through our conflicts. And, ultimately, that we're able to make the right decisions and achieve some positive results."

The table had grown quiet.

"I just want to say how impressed I am at what we've been able to accomplish in a short period of time," I continued. "Anything may happen tomorrow. We all know that. FlyingFox may not be approved by the steering committee."

"We'll build it anyway!" bellowed Wesley, who was working on his third glass of champagne. More laughter.

"Eight months ago, most of us had not worked together. Many of us didn't even know each other."

"Some of us didn't even *like* each other!" added Wesley. He threw his arm around Nick Yu's shoulders, and pressed his cheek affectionately against his shoulder. Everybody howled.

"But think of the advances we've made," I said, while Nick made a mock-disgusted face and unwrapped Wesley's arm. "We've managed to create a team composed of people from very different disciplines, people who speak almost completely different languages."

"Don't talk about Hartmut that way," called Nick. "Not everyone was born an American."

"I was born a designer!" declared Hartmut.

I gestured to Hartmut. "We've brought in a whole new group from the outside, and managed to work with them although we seldom see them and they're based half a continent away."

"A little too close at that," added Wesley, his glass being refilled once again.

Andrea and Keith, sitting together, shook their heads in despair at the adolescent behavior of their teammates.

"Plus, we've already solved some tough issues together. When we first looked at FlyingFox a few months ago—and I think Nick would agree—it was little more than a good idea and a jumble of components. Today, we've got a good working model that is manufacturable. And, by the rumors I'm hearing from the field, I'm beginning to think we may even have a leap-frogger. FlyingFox could take us a jump ahead of MarTech. And that could mean a real turnaround for FCI in the marketplace. If so, we'd be responsible."

"Hail to the Foxes!" said a familiar voice. We all turned. Jasper had poked his head in the door. He surveyed the room and noticed the magnum of champagne currently hovering over Hartmut's glass. "Hmm, I see we're treating ourselves rather well," he said, just a hint of feigned shock and disapproval in his voice.

"You're not actually seeing me here," he said, stepping into the room. "But I think you should know that if I *were* here, even though I'm not, I would probably leak to you, although not in an official capacity, that FlyingFox has been approved and funded."

His message was convoluted enough that we took a moment to realize what he was telling us.

"That is to say," he said, "that it would be wrong of me to break the good news to you tonight, since you're not supposed to be officially notified until tomorrow. But I just hate to see good champagne being drunk without a proper celebration to go with it."

He ran his hand over his head, raised his eyebrows. "My, I'm thirsty. That was a long day we had."

Hartmut seized the moment. "Get the man a glass!" he bellowed, and a second later Jasper was raising his filled goblet in a toast.

"To FlyingFox!" he said.

"FlyingFox!" we all echoed.

Jasper drained his glass. "Just don't screw it up now," he said. And then he was gone.

We watched the door close. And then there was a spontaneous, tremendous "YES!" from all concerned.

It isn't cheap treating ten people to dinner, providing them with their fill of vintage champagne and specially prepared hors d'oeuvres. As the dinner wound to a close, Hartmut and I began an elaborate waltz for the check. We were sitting side by side, and a waiter had strategically placed the check at a neutral point equidistant between us. I had assumed, since Hartmut had made the reservation and had even spoken to the chef, that the meal was on Shark. A generous thank you to FCI for our business.

But one by one, the team members left the table, and still Hartmut did not pick up the check. Finally, I looked at him purposefully. He flashed his most charming smile at me. "An excellent meal, Ron." I decided this was not the time or place to make an issue of a relatively small amount of money—although I winced at the $1,482 bottom line (before tip) as I signed it to my room.

I made a late-night, wine-soaked mental note: Make sure to get agreement on all financial aspects of the deal with your outside partners before you begin work. Above all: Avoid surprises.

As I wandered through the lobby on the way back to my room, I bumped into Dick Eggart.

"Ronnie!"

He was in high spirits, clutching a tumbler of bourbon.

"How'd your presentation go, Ronnie?"

"Very well, Dick. How about yours?"

"These presentations don't mean anything, you know that, Ronnie. That's not how they decide."

"What do you mean?"

"Ron, Ron, Ron. It's not the presentation, it's whether they *like* you or not. That's what it's all about." Dick playfully punched me on the arm and headed off toward the lobby bar. I saw him join a table of Fickies, not one of whom was a member of his Ficus team. By contrast, a small group of diehard Foxes had moved their celebration into the bar. Hartmut and Phyllis sat at a table talking; Andrea and Keith were dancing on the minuscule parquet floor. I waved at them, but it was a slow dance and the last thing on their minds was their Tall Team Leader.

I was rummaging for my room key when I heard someone rushing up behind me.

"Hi, Ron." It was Phyllis. "Ron," she said, earnestly, "I just want to thank you for that note you sent me a few weeks ago." Her eyes were watery. "It was very thoughtful of you to send it. And I truly appreciate it. It was the most sincere and genuine compliment I have ever received in all my years at FCI. I can't tell you how much that means to me."

"Well, Phyllis . . ." I began, with genuine affection for her. "I . . ."

"And I wanted to tell you, too, that I think you're doing an excellent job." She chuckled. "I have to confess that I thought you were a spy or something when you first came to talk with me."

"Why?"

"I don't know, there's always some management consultant snooping around trying to measure our productivity or streamline our process or something like that. I mean, I couldn't imagine that anybody would want a purchasing person on a product development team."

"Well—"

"I just hope I can continue to make a contribution." She paused, then changed her tone. "But Ron, what happens to the team after FlyingFox is launched?" I pictured Phyllis stuck within the halls of vacation posters forever, nickling and diming and never being asked her opinion of anything again.

"I don't know yet, Phyllis. The team may be disbanded, or perhaps we'll have another assignment. But whatever happens, I'll do everything I can to get you in a position where your talents are put to good use and appreciated. Your contribution to the team won't be forgotten."

"Thanks, Ron." She smiled broadly. "Time to get back to the celebration. I'm so glad Barry isn't here. He never stays up this late!"

I powered up the laptop before falling into bed.

FOXFILE ENTRY:

- Success. Trust. Working successfully through conflicts. And perhaps most significant, team members beginning to want to perpetuate the team's success. Team FlyingFox is, I believe, truly a *performing* team.

42. *We Assess Ourselves.*

We got the official word of approval Sunday morning and spent the rest of the day closeted with the four successful New World teams, presenting our programs to each other. Three projects had not made the cut, however, and Ficus was one of them. I must admit that its failure bolstered my belief in the New World process.

I had run into Dick Eggart that morning at breakfast. He was looking headachy and miserable.

"How are you feeling this morning, Dick?"

"Betrayed."

"Why?"

He looked at me sideways.

"Let's put it this way. I was led to believe that Ficus would be approved."

"How did your presentation go?"

"Who cares." Dick shrugged. "I think they just wanted to make an example of me."

"What do you mean?"

"You know I don't go along with all this teamwork and empowerment crap. So they let me volunteer as corporate team leader, I go down in flames, and it proves their point. They set me up."

"Who is they?"

"They. Ferry and his little in-group. You know who I mean. It's not my friends. They wouldn't do this to me."

Dick's eggs benedict and bloody mary arrived, and I left him in peace to spin his conspiracy theories.

The teams stayed on at The Woods through Monday. Team FlyingFox convened to work through a series of issues that had been presented to us by the steering committee, chew over the feedback we had gotten from the other teams, and also review our progress on the three corporate "vitals." Hartmut and Keith had returned home, and Cub was on the road. He joined us periodically during the meeting, however, by telephone from his car. After the euphoria of Saturday night and Sunday afternoon, we now found ourselves facing the most difficult test of all: building our product and getting it to the market. Selling it.

At the end of the meeting we turned to a discussion of our teamwork. How were we doing? Were there any issues to be discussed? What challenges did we face in the months ahead?

Nelson poked a finger in the air. "Well, I'm losing my manager. So I'm wondering who I'll be reporting to now."

Kate's ears pricked up; it was not yet general knowledge that Carlos was leaving. "What do you mean you're losing your manager? Are you talking about Carlos?"

Nelson shrunk into his chair. "Yes," he said, looking at me.

"Wait a minute," said Kate, challenge in her voice. "You're telling me that you're going to produce this new machine without the supervision of our most senior manufacturing person?"

I began to hope that this might force Kate out of the team altogether. "Yes," I said, with no apology.

"I can't believe this," she said. "Why didn't you tell me? Does Zanoski know this? Does Jasper know this?"

"Jasper knows," I told her.

"But you didn't tell the steering committee yesterday. You let them believe that Carlos was still with us."

"Nelson spoke for manufacturing. He'll be in charge of the project from now on."

"Well, good luck to you, Nelson, you're going to need it. You know perfectly well what happens when the head manufacturing guy leaves."

Nelson decided not to allow Kate to disparage his plant. "No, what happens?"

Kate leered at him. "Gremlins happen. Your factory is going to fill up with nasty little creatures that you can't control and they're going to screw up every machine in sight. You'll be lucky if you get one FlyingFox out the door by the deadline."

I was impressed by Nelson's ability to stay calm in the face of Kate's attack. "I don't think that's going to happen. We're already producing product with as much as 85 percent from actual production tooling."

Kate stood and flailed her arms. "Plus, you're dealing with designers who don't know the plant at all. Who knows what else these Shark people are going to cook up, and who knows if you can build it? Am I right, Wesley?"

Wesley shook his head. "No. You're not right. They've been conscientious about design for manufacture. Our electronic hookup has helped us speed up the review and approval process between design, engineering, management, and manufacturing. No, I don't think that will be a problem."

"We'll see," Kate said ominously. She turned to me again. "Ron, this is probably against your precious ground rules, but we are talking about teamwork, so I want to bring up these Shark people. I spent some time talking with Keith and Hartmut yesterday, and they seem eager to be involved in the identity materials and logo design for FlyingFox."

"That's part of the design task," said Nick, in Shark's defense.

"Not where I come from," Kate snapped. "That's the province of my people, working with the ad agency. We have an excellent track record there, and I don't think we should be spending a lot of money on Shark when we can do a better job in-house. I don't think they have the expertise to pull it off, and besides, it's too risky."

"What do you mean, too risky?" asked Andrea. Andrea and Kate's relationship had been growing strained as the weeks went along.

"You know as well as I do that Shark has their own agenda, and it's not about making FlyingFox the best product it can be for FCI. They want a showpiece, and they don't really care if it meets the requirements of our customers."

"That is absolute crap," said Andrea. "What proof do you have of that?"

"Experience," Kate said, haughtily. "I've worked with enough design firms and agencies to recognize the symptoms. Hartmut wants to see his picture in the trade magazines. He wants to win the big national awards. That pulls in more business for Shark, and it feeds his rather bigger-than-life ego. Besides, he usually works with smaller companies than FCI. FlyingFox is a coup for him and he wants to milk us for all we're worth."

"I haven't observed the kind of behavior you're talking about with Shark," I said. "I think we're all happy with the design. And, as far as I can tell, the working relationship is successful. Remember, part of their compensation comes from profits, not fees. It's in Shark's interest for FlyingFox to be a commercial success."

I looked at Wesley, Nick, and Nelson for confirmation.

Wesley spoke up. "Kate, you're out of line on this. You haven't worked with them. Hartmut may have a big ego—which is not unusual, I've noticed, in the marketing world either—but he's good to work with. The guy knows his stuff and so does Keith. FlyingFox is a better product than we could have made it without them. I'm sure of that."

Kate glowered at Wesley.

"The real issue," said Andrea, "is focusing on the market now. We don't have the beginnings of a marketing plan."

"We're starting next week," said Kate. She looked at me. "We've booked a meeting, right, Ron?" We hadn't, although that was the plan.

"No one told me about it," objected Andrea. "I should be in that meeting, too."

"You're welcome to sit in," Kate said, as if speaking to an unwanted child.

By this time Kate had insulted virtually everybody in the group, and she was threatening to poison the whole meeting.

"I suggest that you and I discuss some of these issues after this meeting, Kate. I know you have concerns about Hartmut, and I don't want you to continue on in the team unless you're comfortable with the team members."

Kate wagged her head as if to say okay. But she wasn't happy.

Later, in search of advice, I took advantage of The Woods' business center to send an E-mail.

To: Martha
From: Ron

At what point do you decide that a team member should no longer be a team member? Kate simply is not committed. She is primarily concerned about her own status, and shifts her allegiances with each day. We're not going to get the effort out of her we should. FlyingFox will suffer, and she'll say I told you so.

To: Ron
From: Martha

If you have serious doubts, discuss them with her now. Make sure you have thought through your position, however. Did you state your expectations clearly enough to really be sure that she hasn't met them? Are you better off with her partial commitment than you are without her completely? How will the other members of the team respond? Who will take her place?

43. *Separation Anxiety.*

Late that afternoon, Kate and I convened in The Woods' bar. Kate ordered her beloved Campari and soda and, just out of contrariness, I ordered the same thing.

"Is there a message here, Ron? You're starting to see things my way?" asked Kate, and I remembered the first TSG staff meeting, when I had sat in her chair. I thought: Listen to her. Listen. Maybe you have an attitude toward her that you're not aware of.

We were sitting on the nearly empty patio, which over-looked a broad field that ended in the pine woods of the state forest. Kate, with her blond hair, looked particularly striking against the deep green-black of the trees. Neither of us was in the mood for speaking in the veiled language of corporate non-confrontation. I wanted to get to the bottom of her attitude toward FlyingFox and me, and I was prepared to ask her to leave the team if it came to that. Andrea could take over.

"Kate, look. Bill Ferry said that teamwork was to be consid-ered a condition of employment at FCI from now on."

"So he did." She sipped on her Campari.

"I think he was clear on that point. And you are theoreti-cally a part of the FlyingFox team. But it's obvious that you're not a contributing member."

"Ron, I can't say it in any new way: I'll do my job, and I'll do it well. When it's time. In the meantime, Ron, *you're* the voice of marketing."

"My background is marketing, but my primary role is proj-ect manager. Team leader."

"Fine. But you bring the marketing perspective to the party already. We don't need two of us doing the same thing."

She had never said that she considered me as the key mar-keting person. Perhaps she had simply been respecting my turf all along.

"Then why did you participate at all?" I asked.

"I see my major responsibility as the launch. The commu-nications part. I wanted to get involved early and that's what I did. Not to develop plans and make presentations, but so I could understand what FlyingFox is all about. And that's just what I have done. Now I won't have to get up to speed in a hurry when you need my services, because I'm up to speed already. That will save us time. We'll get to market faster. I mean, earlier. And that is an improvement over the old way of doing things."

This made sense. "But—"

"You keep pushing at me, Ron, and I don't know why."

"I had the impression I was always being pushed by you."

"I'm the one who volunteered for this team. Remember?"

"Yes, but—"

"You thought I had my own agenda. You even thought I was leaking secrets out in the field. What have you got against me? That I'm ambitious?"

"I have nothing against you," I protested. "It's just that I always feel you're more concerned with the politics of a situation than you are about the real issues at hand. At the session this morning you insulted virtually everybody in the room. You were intolerant and arrogant."

"Ron, listen. If teamwork means having to put up with the whining of a bunch of Fickie lifers, starry-eyed kids, and outside egomaniacs with no sense of the real world of business, then I think it's a massive waste of time. I have people that I trust to carry out the work and whom I work well with. I don't want to deal with these endless meanderings about 'Oh, who do I report to? How do I get evaluated?' Just hand the work over to me and let's get on with it."

I shook my head. "Some of that meandering is inevitable. You just have to deal with it, and try to keep it in balance with the tasks at hand."

"It may be inevitable for you, but not for me. I'm not interested in all that. I'm interested in the product."

"You don't show it much."

Kate reeled backward. She cocked her head at me, then spoke in a lower tone. "Ron. You don't get it, do you? I don't *want* to look too enthusiastic about any one product. That's a way to limit myself, and probably get in deep trouble. I've got to keep myself on a much higher plane. That's the only way I'm going to keep moving up, and through the damned Fickie glass ceiling. I don't want to be seen as a gushy product manager. I want to be seen as a global thinker and corporate strategist."

"But not a team player."

She shook her head. "I'm doing my best, Ron. I know you don't believe it, but I'm doing my best to play with your team. You just don't want my contribution."

"I keep telling you that I do."

"Case in point. That marketing research data I brought to the rehearsal. No one showed a scintilla of interest."

"Your timing was rotten."

"No one has asked me a thing about it in the three days we've been up here."

I said nothing. I was picturing Kate maneuvering through the mazes of corporate hierarchy, always shifting from one corridor to another, never allowing herself to stay or be seen in one place for too long. Keeping moving was her key to upward mobility. Her whole approach was antithetical to teamwork. But she was trying. I couldn't kick her off the team yet. It would send a bad signal to the rest of the company: Teams can be ugly; teams are just as nasty as the old hierarchy. Besides, she probably wouldn't let me.

Kate noticed our CFO and a member of the steering committee coming into the bar. She smiled at me as if nothing had happened.

"See you later, Ron."

She threaded her way through the umbrellaed tables and caught up with our CFO. Within twenty seconds, they were deep in conversation.

44. *I Engage in Much-Needed R&R.*

After I left Kate, I went back to my room and lay down on the bed. I was expecting Janice in an hour or so; we had planned to take a couple of days off, to stay at The Woods and attempt to relax. The kids were staying with their grandmother.

As soon as the quilted coverlet began to impress its patterns into my back, I could feel the electrons snap and crackle out of my brain—the amassed impressions and concerns, memories and images of the past months.

We had successfully passed a milestone. The judgment at Judgment Day had gone for us. Whatever lay ahead, I felt—at that moment, anyway—that we could and would prevail. Manufacturing problems, marketing challenges, Kate, Jasper, Ferry, evaluation, compensation, FungiFlex, Zanoski, MarTech, trade shows, rumors, technology, database security, Mercedes coupes, software glitches . . .

A knocking startled me out of my half-sleep and I stumbled to answer the door. In my condition, Janice looked to me like a person from another life, welcome but unfamiliar. I shook my head, trying to regain my grasp on the moment.

"Uh-oh," she said. "You didn't get approved?"

I snapped alert. "Yes! Yes, we did. Fully funded."

Janice closed the door behind her. "So that means we can actually afford this holiday?"

I laughed. "The room's already paid for."

She took my hands. "Let's start using it then, for heaven's sake. When did we last get two days alone, without the kids, in a free hotel room?" She kicked off her shoes.

I thought of the distant and intense days when Janice and I were first going out, and then flashed on last night's lingering image of Keith and Andrea pressed together on the dance floor. I was suddenly overwhelmed by the powerful sense of caring deeply about another person. Janice and I enjoyed The Woods so much that we extended our stay. FlyingFox could live without me for one more day. I hoped.

Part III

45. *The Future Looms.*

As fall waned into winter, the realization of what we had to accomplish grew increasingly intense. Our schedule called for public launch of FlyingFox in early spring. If we thought we had been working flat out prior to Judgment Day, we now learned that we could be far busier.

Kate, true to her word, went into action, and within a few weeks we began evaluating her striking promotional concepts and logo graphics, preparing a media schedule, and planning the launch and other public relations events. Kate handed Andrea a lot of responsibility, particularly for public relations and the launch events themselves, and Andrea immediately blossomed into the role.

Kate, I had to admit, had been right about her approach and her abilities. With the project funded and the product in workable form, with its rich green FungiFlex housing, we were able to concentrate properly on the marketing issues. I had had a case of cross-functional ignorance. Because I hadn't truly understood Kate's role, I had been nervous. I had wanted to see action just for the sake of action. In short, I hadn't trusted Kate. But, in my defense, she hadn't made it easy to trust her.

FlyingFox was in pilot production, and several FlyingFox machines were humming away at beta sites. The Nick-Wesley-Shark-Nelson axis was working together well. They were nestled into their own little computer network and could chatter happily away, sharing data and drawings, wherever they happened to find themselves.

As we neared Start of Production, we added two new partner firms—one a supplier of a key subcomponent, and the other a raw-materials supplier. The network widened and, having overcome our initial nervousness with long-distance relationships, the partnerships flourished. Having learned our lesson, we kept MIS informed and had no more confrontations on the issue of network security.

FungiFlex, despite some inevitable manufacturing glitches, was proving to be a material with superb potential. The rest of the FCI organization got wind of it almost immedi-

177

ately, and several managers were considering it for their new projects. Zanoski was a changed man. Receiving accolades from within and sensing a commercial hit on his hands, he became less stern and aloof and his natural charm was more pronounced. He became a valued team member, although seldom physically in evidence.

Carlos was gone, and we'd heard nothing from him. Andrea spent a good deal of her time shuttling back and forth between Building Three and Shark's headquarters, working closely with Keith and Hartmut on FlyingFox identity materials. Phyllis, working with her manager, had managed to cut several unnecessary steps out of the PO approval process, reducing the average time from request to signature almost in half. Nick was working too many hours and looked tired.

Our contact with the steering committee was now limited to irregular meetings between Jasper and me. At one of these, only six weeks before the launch, we strayed from our normal discussion of plans and programs and specific issues. Jasper sat back, holding his beloved wooden skull. He pointed at the SPEECH zone.

"Sometimes it seems that successful teamwork is little more than successful communications," he mused.

"That's certainly a major part of it," I agreed.

"Look at what you've accomplished to date. Much of what you've done is to improve communications among people who had substantial barriers to communication built into the structure of the organization. You have your regular meetings. Your team room, for example, which, by the way, the buildings manager says I am supposed to reprimand you about for claiming without proper authorization."

"I stand chastised."

"Your computer link with Shark and manufacturing and these new partner firms. This electronic FoxFile that I often dip into with interest."

"It's all simple stuff. What gets communicated is the difficult part."

"But that's harder to affect, and it's a function of the skills and abilities of your people."

"Yeah, that's why I'd say casting is the most important element of team building. Choosing the right people and then helping them to contribute as best they can."

"And you've had your share of issues to contend with in that regard."

We had never discussed Carlos' leaving or my difficulties with Kate. The unwritten FCI code dictates that you never criticize a colleague—at least not in a way that seems to be criticism, and certainly never in public.

Jasper went to his desk and rummaged through a drawer. "What do you think of Kate's performance so far? I'm looking for some honest evaluation of her performance, from your perspective as a team leader."

"She's not easy to work with. But she's smart. And she knows what she's doing. She just has no tolerance for anything she sees as irrelevant. She's not exactly a cross-functional team player."

Jasper scratched his chin.

"Why do you ask?"

He looked at me thoughtfully. "She's up for a vice-presidency."

"I see. When would that happen?"

"Not decided." Jasper changed the subject. "Now let me ask you this. How do you see yourself after the FlyingFox launch?"

I had not thought that far ahead. "Probably dead."

"Oh, that's just prelaunch wishful thinking. But try to keep it on the optimistic side. If you had your choice, would you be more comfortable returning to the hierarchical style of the Old World? Or would you rather keep the FlyingFox team intact? Maybe restructure it a little and take on a new challenge?"

"Why do you ask, Jasper? Do you have some even more risky project in mind for me?"

Mock astonishment. "Ron. Please. Remember this is the New World. We're trying to bring teamwork into every level of the organization. That means working as colleagues to figure out what our structure should be. That means each team leader helping to shape the very mission of the corporation."

"Do you believe that's possible?"

Jasper wagged his head. "Ferry believes it's possible and I respect his opinion. So, to the point, what's your answer?"

I had not thought about the pre-FlyingFox days recently. They were long ago enough now for me to think of them as the past. And, as soon as the first images came into my head—of bored meetings, suffering projects, endless approval cycles, jealous glances at the competition, jockeying for corporate position—I knew that I did not wish to go back.

"I know one thing. I'd be much better at developing a team next time."

"What would you do differently?"

"I wouldn't worry so much about everybody's total commitment, and just make sure I had the *right* commitment from each person. I had trouble with Kate, for example, because I was asking her to work in a way that suited me, not her. Zanoski is a valued team member and didn't attend a single staff meeting. We seldom see Cub, but he's a contributing member. The Shark people are in a different time zone, and we feel close to them.

"My point is that a team like ours is not a place, even if we do have the Lair. It's not even a total way of life. It's not a work group like the kind you have on an assembly line or something. It's more amorphous and elastic."

"Which makes it harder to manage."

"Different to manage. If you can't break out of the traditional command and control techniques, you're probably going to go crazy. Simply as a practical matter, there is no way you can keep tabs on people you don't see and don't necessarily evaluate. It won't work. It can't work."

"So what do you think holds the team together?"

"I suppose it's commitment." I considered FlyingFox. "Over time, we have come to believe that FlyingFox is going to be a good product. We believe in the process we're using; it works. We've come to trust each other, even enjoy each other, so there are rewards and benefits in the everyday working life. Short-term stuff. But," I continued, "we don't yet have the luxury of long-term success. I think if that were the case, like Martha's C&P Group, we'd also have some pride of accomplishment and outside recognition to keep us together."

"True," said Jasper, sitting down again. "Now, what about

our performance," he said, gulping theatrically. "My, this hurts to ask. Do you think you've gotten the support from senior management that you need? From Ferry. From the steering committee." He closed his eyes, as if in prayer. "From me?"

A question *never* heard in the Old World.

"I find you to be perfect, Jasper. Every day in every way."

Jasper breathed a mock sigh of relief. "Excellent answer, Ron. But, really now. Senior managers have to play their role. It's our role to establish the vision and set some goals. We should keep an eye on things, to make sure those goals are being met. And we ought to be able to redirect those efforts which are not serving the goals." He paused.

"Yes," I said.

"Ron, don't make this difficult. Do you think we've been doing that at FCI? And, if not, what could we be doing better?"

"The goals were clearly set. You and the steering committee have been reasonably accessible. Ferry, too. Given the constraints of time, and all the rest."

"But . . . ?"

"The one intangible—and this is something that Andrea brings up all the time—is what long-term effect our participation on this team will have on our jobs and our position within the company. Do we get paid more? Do we get more authority? Do we get a better office? Will I ever get to be vice-president? Or does a successful team leader remain a team leader forever?"

"Yes," said Jasper, thoughtfully. "And those are questions we don't know the answers to. What everybody has to realize is that the company is *changing.* We don't know exactly what kind of effect on time to market, competitiveness, the bottom line—all that important stuff—working in teams is going to have. That's what the New World people are all about. You're the beta teams, the pioneers."

"Our job is to go out into the wilderness and establish a colony."

Jasper nodded unapologetically. "That's right. All I can say is that it's our intention that you *will* be properly recognized. You will be rewarded. I think your work will change the fabric of the organization for the better, and it'll be good for the team members as individuals, as well. You included, team leader."

"Thanks, Jasper."

"Oh, and by way of praise and commendation, I want you to know that Ferry is very high on your group. He talks about Team FlyingFox a lot."

"To whom?"

"Anybody who will listen. You know how lonely it is at the top."

46. *I Feel Validated.*

That afternoon I got an unexpected telephone call from Donnell Ware. When he first said his name, I drew a blank, and then I remembered the former colleague whom Cub and I had bumped into at the IOTSF trade show.

"Hey, Ron!" he began. "You guys are all the talk of the industry these days."

"FCI?"

"No. Your group. FlyingFox. Isn't that what you call it?"

I didn't want to be the talk of the industry. Especially if Donnell was doing the talking.

"Everybody at MarTech is wringing their hands over this new product of yours," he went on.

Andrea's skillful public relations work had gotten us good trade press, without spilling many details about FlyingFox.

"Well, Donnell, you are the competition and that's part of our job, to keep you nervous."

"Don't worry. I'm not looking for information, Ron." His voice grew confidential. "In fact, I'm looking for an opportunity."

"A job?"

"Correct."

I almost whooped with glee. A MarTech person—progressive, youthful, market-busting MarTech—wanting to come to work for stodgy, old, losing-its-edge FCI. "Have you talked to the HR people?" I asked.

"Ron, I'm wondering about your team. You're about ready to introduce your product, right? You're going to need some more help in the field, I bet."

"I can give you the name of the salesperson to talk with."

"But don't you do the hiring and firing?"

"Tell you the truth, Donnell, I haven't hired anybody yet for this team except for some temps. I've recruited everybody from within the company. So I'm not sure exactly who would make that hiring decision."

"You're kidding me." Donnell did not know how to proceed. "Well, how about if we have a drink or dinner or something, so we could talk some more?"

"What's wrong with MarTech? Why are you leaving?"

Donnell's voice, which had returned to a normal level, dropped again. "It's chaos, Ron. Everybody is running around with no idea of what is going on. There's no organization. There's no hierarchy at all. I mean the flat organization is fine and all that. Empowerment is great, but come on, you need a little stability in your life."

"I'm not sure that FCI is going to be the right place for you then. Our cross-functional team structure is not exactly a traditional hierarchy."

"I understand how teams work. I'm just looking to slow down a little bit, spend more time on the important stuff. I'd like to find a company that thinks before it acts."

It sounded to me as if Donnell were looking for a retirement plan, not a new job. "We're trying to shorten our time to market. So I'm not sure you'd slow down here."

Donnell paused. "I guess I didn't mean slow down, exactly. It's just that these smaller companies don't have the resources to support a good sales effort. There's too much seat-of-the-pants stuff. We don't even have an assistant at our branch office. When I need something, I basically have to get it myself."

"FCI may be bigger. But I'm not sure you'd have that much more support here, Donnell. We're trying to become more like MarTech. Faster and more flexible."

A whine crept into Donnell's voice. "Hey, Ron. I'm willing to play it any way that works for you. It's just that I think of myself as a winner, and I want to align myself with winners. Couldn't we just get together and talk for a while? I'd love to buy you—"

"Sure," I said. "But why don't you talk to our sales guy first."

I gave Donnell Cub's number. I don't think he even wrote it down.

"Okay, great, thanks," Donnell said weakly. "Of course, I'd rather deal with you. If you're out my way, make sure you give me a call."

"Maybe you should stay with MarTech, Donnell. I think they're a good strong company."

"Oh, of course, they're dying to keep me." Donnell's voice was growing fainter. "Nice talking with you, Ron."

I hung up. In the old days, I probably would have set up a bunch of interviews for Donnell, squandered too much time and effort on somebody who had openly confessed that he was looking to slow down and work a little less hard. But Donnell did not meet the profile I wanted for New World Fickies. At least he hadn't called me Red.

FOXFILE ENTRY:

• Team FlyingFox is a little famous within the Fick. Now, I find fewer occasions where I seek outside advice from Martha and others. In fact, other Fickies are seeking advice and guidance from us. We are regularly getting requests from insiders who want to join the team.

In light of so much positive recognition, the challenge for us is to keep our eyes on the task. Team FlyingFox might be performing well, but Product FlyingFox is nothing yet. That realization is helping to keep us humble.

47. *We Receive Disturbing News.*

At our regular Wednesday staff meeting in early March, we reviewed plans for the launch event. The Wednesday meetings, in general, were well attended. Those who could not attend were asked to notify somebody who was planning to be there, leave a note in the file, or stick a note on the Lair whiteboard. One of us always kept minutes, usually entering them into the quietest laptop we could find, and the minutes were distributed to all the team members electronically.

We joked about the number of ways people could attend the meeting, apart from showing up in the flesh. Cub was usually on the speaker phone. We held the meeting as a videoconference whenever we wanted the Shark people in on a decision. Now and again Nelson would attend on-line, reading the meeting notes as they were entered by the designated notetaker (a task we shared in rotation) and sometimes responding with a note.

As we had grown more comfortable with each other, it came to matter less and less *how* we communicated, so long as we did communicate. Fax. Voice mail. File. Telephone. Face to face. It wasn't that any single technology held a secret to improved communications, but that every technology enabled communications between team members at different times and in different places.

That technology enables communications is not, of course, news. But what I began to understand more clearly as FlyingFox matured was that technology was equally capable of stifling teamwork—and that was just what it had been doing in the Old World. In the preteam days, we had become so convinced of the benefits of computing and electronic communications that we often overlooked other, simpler working methods. If the network went down, our day was shot. If we had a process problem, we looked for a new application to purchase that could automate it.

In Team FlyingFox, we viewed computers as useful tools, but they came second to people.

At that Wednesday morning meeting, however, Phyllis (who had become our unofficial MIS manager) made a triumphant announcement of a new technological breakthrough— laptops for the sales force.

"We now are able to integrate the sales and marketing database with the inventory, ordering, and customer service database," Phyllis reported.

Cub whooped. "Fanfoxingtastic! I nominate this lady for a FlyingFox pelt!"

The FlyingFox pelt was a verbal pat on the back, the highest honor in our informal reward system. You could be nominated to receive a pelt by anyone on the team, but had to be approved by a majority of the members. Pelt receivers were duly noted in the FoxFile.

"No, I don't deserve a pelt for this." Phyllis smiled modestly. It also was acceptable, even expected, that team members would decline the pelt if they felt unworthy, or elect to share it with someone else who had contributed to the effort.

Next, Andrea outlined the elements of the launch—from early press coverage (already begun) to beta-site testing (in the works), to sales force event and public launch, including advertising and special promotions. Andrea got high marks for her work, which had been supported by a group of agencies and vendors she had assembled with Kate's help. But feelings ran high about the sales force launch itself. The plan, as it stood, was to introduce FlyingFox to the sales force as part of the regular sales and management meeting.

"The problem with that," Cub began, "is that all the salespeople won't be there. It's just the regional managers. And we need to get the word out to everybody."

Throughout the morning, Wesley had been silent. When we began discussing the launch, he twitched.

"Wesley, what's your view on the launch event?" I asked.

"I think we'll have to push it back."

Everybody stared at Wesley.

"Why?"

"We're not going to be ready." Wesley was miserable.

"What are you talking about?"

"We've got a problem." Wesley looked at Nelson and Nick, who were also staring down at the table.

We were right up against our launch deadline, and I had assured Jasper and the steering committee that we would launch at the management meeting in early April. I felt angry and concerned.

"Let's hear it. The only way we're going to fix it is to get it on the table," I said.

Wesley sighed again. "We've got a software glitch."

"Can't we fix it?" asked Andrea.

"We've tried to fix it," said Wesley.

"Does Shark know about it?" I asked.

"They're the ones who found it. Just before the Woods meeting."

I remembered Hartmut's mention of a glitch. "What's the cause of the problem? How serious is it?" I asked.

Wesley half smiled. "It affects the voice response system.

Sometimes it will misunderstand a command and do the wrong thing." Incomprehensibly, he giggled.

"Why is that funny?" I wondered.

Wesley looked at Nick. And now Nick snorted, as if trying to control an uncontrollable eruption of laughter.

"It also," continued Wesley, "sometimes affects the words the machine says."

"It told me to shove it." Nick giggled.

I couldn't believe this was happening. This was a serious flaw in the system, it threatened our launch date, and our product people were laughing about it.

"Why didn't you tell us about it?" I asked.

"The problem is intermittent. At first we thought it was an aberration, and would not recur. Then we were sure we could fix it. We didn't want to get the team all worried about something they couldn't really contribute to. Finally, we just ran out of time," said Nick.

The team sat in silence. I remembered the day that Nick had first shown FlyingFox to me in the basement, and that it had said it was "teddy" rather than "ready." So this was an old and chronic problem. And possibly a fatal one.

"Have you spoken to Zanoski about it?"

"No," said Nick.

"We didn't want to lose control of the project," said Wesley.

FlyingFox had given these two responsibility and ownership. They didn't want to give it up. Their loyalty and enthusiasm, however, had led to protectionism and secrecy. Trying to focus on the problem, I looked at the faces strewn around the Lair. Everyone had forgotten about ground rules, meeting behavior, methods of brainstorming, and thinking techniques. No one raced to the flipchart to list objectives or issues. No one cracked a joke to lighten our mood. We sat in a funk. Finally, Cub broke the silence from the speaker phone.

"Come on, let's think of something! Ron, you told me we had the best brains in the company on this stupid team. We have to get FlyingFox out in the field. I've got my commissions to think of! Come on, people."

Just as it had at our first rehearsal, Cub's call to action galvanized the team. Suddenly, we all were talking at once. I scribbled the ideas on the board, as they were articulated:

> Remove the voice response and offer it as an option later.
> Delay the launch, but announce the product.
> Hire a software specialist firm to help.
> Get Zanoski involved.
> Announce FlyingFox on a trial basis.
> Present the problem to steering committee/senior managers.
> Establish a plan to replace defective units.

Once the list was complete, we debated and discussed each idea, but we could not make ourselves satisfied with any solution. It was Nelson who, in his calm, considered way, suggested Jocelyn.

"Listen. I happen to know that Jocelyn is planning to install an advanced voice response telephone system for FCI. Maybe she can help, or knows someone who can."

We considered this. I could sense the internal debate; we needed help, but we had an old bone to pick with Jocelyn over her threat to cut our connection with Shark. Old animosities die hard.

"I suggest we start with MIS," I said finally. "It's our cheapest, simplest, most available solution. And it doesn't cut off any of the other options."

We finally reached a consensus. Jocelyn got a second chance with Team FlyingFox.

48. *In Search of Software Excellence.*

Jocelyn received us graciously.

"How can I help you?" She looked at me, as the team leader, but we had elected Wesley as our spokesperson.

"We've run into a software problem that we can't solve with our internal resources, especially considering our deadline," began Wesley. He paused. I could see a light come on deep in Jocelyn's eyes. Her attitude toward the subject of software obviously was quite different from mine.

"It's an intermittent glitch that seems to be related to . . ." And here Wesley soared off into a language so rich in acronyms and compound nouns that I did not try to follow. However, after no more than six minutes of this, Jocelyn offered a solution.

"Prandar," she said.

The name struck a chord with Wesley. "Of course! Why the hell didn't we think of him?"

"Who is Prandar?" The name was familiar, but I couldn't place it.

"He's that software genius. He used to be in the old TS division, but now he's sort of an FCI free agent. He roams around the organization looking for the most complicated, impossible, high-risk problems he can find," said Wesley.

"We worked together recently," added Jocelyn. "I should warn you that his working methods are bizarre. He's not going to come over and attend your staff meetings. You may find him hard to communicate with. But if anybody can solve your problem, he can."

"What do you mean, come over? Where is he based?" I asked.

"He keeps an office in our Paris facility. And he sometimes hangs out in the Birmingham plant, in the U.K. But he could be anywhere. California. Dallas. Vancouver."

"Who does he report to? Who's his manager?" I asked in all innocence.

"Prandar has no manager. He reports to the goddess of software," said Jocelyn. "It took me three days to locate him last time I tried. He hates E-mail. He hates fax. He prefers to talk on-line."

"You mean real-time computer connection?" Wesley asked.

"He's always got a laptop or a notebook with him, and he always figures out a way to access the network."

The task of locating Prandar fell to Phyllis. I didn't want to distract Wesley and Nick from pursuing their own solutions. Andrea was up to her ears with launch plans. And, besides, Phyllis had volunteered.

It took her six hours to find him. He was in Switzerland, making a presentation to a conference in Geneva. Yes, he had access to the network at a sales office in the city. No, he was not willing to get involved unless he could talk directly with the engineers about the problem. By "talk," he meant via computer and he only could do so early the next morning, before he left for his next appearance (he spent much of his time speaking at industry conferences), scheduled for Lyons, in the south of France. He would be on a train for several hours and would have some time to think about the problem then.

To connect with Prandar in Geneva at six in the morning meant that Wesley and Nick would have to be at the computer keyboard late at night our time.

"I haven't stayed late for work in years," said Wesley. "It'll be a novelty."

"Yeah, you can see how the next generation of engineers do it," said Nick. "You can relive your youth."

"Great," said Wesley. "Besides, there's no one at home to miss me any more."

The next morning, Nick and Wesley stumbled into the Lair at about ten-thirty. They had been on line with Prandar until two-thirty in the morning, when Prandar had abruptly left to catch his train. They had not solved the problem, but now Prandar had the code and the necessary design drawings. Prandar had impressed both Nick and Wesley; they were convinced that if the problem could be solved, he would solve it.

"Why are you so sure?" I asked.

"He's brilliant," said Wesley. "After we got connected, we were having some difficulty in transmitting data. He diagnosed the problem immediately and told us how to fix it."

"And it worked," added Nick.

"Then he kept asking question after question. And he kept scrolling through the code looking for problems."

"He rewrote two instructions that we had always thought were pretty inelegant, on the spot," said Nick.

"So what happens next?"

Wesley shrugged. "We hope he has a productive train ride. And we'll keep working on it ourselves."

"I feel powerless, relying on some guy we hardly know, working on this laptop on a train racing through the French countryside," I said. I also felt a twinge of jealousy. Prandar was in a privileged position—so talented and experienced that he had earned the status of lone contributor. He set his own rules and didn't have to contend with the endless stresses of team dynamics. Then I remembered that I hated software, and relished working with people. I had no desire to be a Lone Ranger.

"Is there any way to get him out of this conference in Lyons so he can come here and work with us?"

"He says that he would love to get out of the conference," said Wesley. "But he's filling in for guess-who."

"The Bald One?"

"You got it."

Jasper was notorious for accepting any and all invitations to speak or appear at industry conferences, especially in pleasant locations at great distances from the home office. Then, if something more appealing or pressing came up, he would cancel at the last minute and coerce some other Fickie into taking his place.

Now I was faced with two decisions. One, should we keep rolling on toward launch, with a potentially serious problem? Two, could we get Prandar over here, or at least get more of his attention?

49. *The Leaders Are Tested.*

I called Jasper, outlined the problem, and basically demanded a meeting. Jasper wanted Ferry to meet with us too, because of his strong engineering background. I took the back stairs, wondering whether the great espousers of corporate teamwork would prove to be team players themselves. Would they support us, or would they throw FlyingFox to the dogs?

They both were there when I arrived, finishing up a discussion about some other issue. I knew Ferry slightly, but this was the first time I had had such close and specific dealings with him.

"Hi, Ron." Ferry rose and shook my hand, smiling. The greeting was friendly.

"Sit down, O Fox Leader." Jasper retained his usual touch

of sarcasm, even with Ferry in the room. A good sign, I thought.

"Tell us about the problem," said Ferry. And so I did.

Ferry said not a word. He listened. Carefully. Jasper, as was his wont, listened while fiddling with his pen. Occasionally he doodled or straightened the crease of his pants.

I finished with a description of our current situation (Prandar, laptop, train), and Ferry sat back. There was complete silence in the room for what seemed like the length of a short career. Finally, Ferry put his hands behind his neck and spoke to the ceiling.

"So, the critical question is whether to go ahead with the launch as planned."

It had seemed to me that there were dozens of issues. But, really, it all came down to that. "Yes, I guess so."

"What's your V-Two point?"

"V-Two?"

"That's the point that an aircraft reaches when its velocity and the remaining quantity of runway indicate you have only two choices open to you: take off or drive off the end of the runway." Ferry was a serious pilot, often flying his own aircraft to customer sites. "I mean, can you give yourself another couple of days to decide?" Ferry was completely focused, unworried.

"Some of the promotional materials we're working on are dated, time sensitive, but to redo them is no big expense. But if we don't introduce FlyingFox at the meeting, there'll be a hole in the agenda."

Ferry leaned forward. "That's not important." He cocked his head at Jasper. "We can always get Jasper to talk a little longer."

"My pleasure," said Jasper.

"What do you think, Jasper?" asked Ferry. "Do you see a problem in postponing the decision?"

Jasper tapped the table with his pencil. "No."

"Why don't you determine your absolute drop-dead point and try to resolve the problem by then," Ferry said to me. "In the meantime, is there anything we can do to help?"

I smiled at Jasper. "Jasper, you're supposed to be in Lyons tomorrow to address that software conference?"

"Good heavens, no," said Jasper, extracting a pocket diary and quickly riffling through its pages. "No, no, I asked someone to go in my place. Let's see, it was . . ." And then he remembered. "Prandar."

"What are the chances of sending someone in his place, and getting Prandar over here?"

"It would be awkward," said Jasper. "Perhaps Prandar could just cancel."

Ferry looked at Jasper uncomprehendingly. "You're tying up our top software guy at some conference when we need him to solve a product problem here?"

"Well." Jasper was not at all happy at being on the spot. "We needed an influential presence there, and I couldn't clear my schedule."

"What have you got on?" asked Ferry.

Jasper looked sheepish. "The customer golf event." Each year we invited key customers and suppliers to a pro-am golf tournament.

Ferry guffawed.

"I'm supposed to be playing with Lee Trevino," said Jasper, weakly, in his own defense. "And a key customer."

Ferry waved his hand. "I'll take your place, Jasper. Why don't you hop on a plane tonight, and let's see if we can get Prandar over here."

Jasper looked at his watch, nervously.

"Teamwork," I said, smiling at him.

Jasper smiled back. But with murder in his eyes.

50. *I Take on a New Role.*

Jasper went to Lyons; Prandar, however, would not come to us. Instead, he scurried to the sales office outside Paris to work on our software code.

All communication with Prandar was via computer, on-line, real-time—from his laptop, connected via modem to the French telephone system, uplinked to a geosynchronous satellite, downlinked to a land station on the East Coast, and zipped via land lines to the maze of optical fibers and copper wires that constituted the FCI network, one of which led to the beige PC with dirty keys that sat on the conference table in the Lair. All within a few milliseconds.

Prandar was stumped, however, after nearly a full day's work. I was sitting beside Nick, when Prandar made a request.

I would like to have the FlyingFox machine here so I can test my solutions more easily. Can you bring it to me?

Nick looked at me.

"Do you think he really needs it?" I asked.

Do you really need the prototype?

Nick typed.

I would not ask for it if I didn't need it,

Prandar replied.

I thought about the complexities of getting the prototype, packing it properly, dealing with shipping to rush it to the airport, getting it through customs, arranging with our Paris sales office to pick it up. Worse, I imagined the effect that just one less than Total Quality–oriented freight handler could have on the health of the FlyingFox prototype by tossing it just a little too roughly onto a conveyor belt or into the back of a truck.

"We could air freight one this afternoon; he'd probably have it by tomorrow night, or the following morning," I said.

We can have it to you by air freight in a day or two,

Nick wrote.

Too late. I am leaving for Canberra tomorrow afternoon.

"Can you fly over tonight?" I asked Nick.

"We have a major manufacturing review with Zanoski tomorrow. I have to be there. It's the only time Zanoski has and we need his advice."

It had to be me. All the other team members were too immersed in their responsibilities. It was the team leader who must shoulder the lowliest task. If Jasper could fly to Lyons, I could go to Paris.

There was one consolation that helped mitigate the frantic last-minute phone calls, packing, arranging children's schedules, and all the rest: I could only book a first-class seat, at that late date. So I ate and drank well as I flew through the night to Paris, FlyingFox neatly parked beneath my seat.

I felt honorable and youthful as I tucked into the cheese and fruit platter.

Ron Delaney. New World Team Leader.

And Messenger Boy.

51. *Midnight Conversation.*

It was an odd, but not unpleasant, sensation to be separated from the team. I had not been traveling much in the past few months, and when I did it usually was with a Fox to some Fox-related destination. This flight provided me with some distance, and distance provided perspective. The very fact that I was the one taking this flight was significant. In the Old World, I would have delegated the journey, especially at such a critical stage of product development, sure that my absence would lead to some irreparable chaos, convinced that somebody would surely screw something up and only I would be able to rectify it.

In the New World, it was different. The work mattered more than Old World status. Of course my position in the first-class cabin, indulging in my second split of champagne, contributed to my satisfaction.

I'm not much of an airplane conversationalist. I prefer working, reading, or resting to trading travel or business tales with seatmates. But the fellow next to me wanted to talk. He was a starchy man, with snowy white shirt, rep tie, and crisp, deep blue pinstripes. He was also wide of body—I would guess that football figured in his background—and he spoke with an underlying aggressiveness in his voice.

"Yeah," said my seatmate, "I finally decided I had better get over to Europe so I could straighten some things out. Sometimes you've got to bang a few heads together to get people moving."

I remembered this attitude. It belonged to a world of bosses and headbangers, lords and vassals.

"Mm," I said.

"This whole business of flattening the organization is fine," he continued, emptying his dish of mixed nuts into a capacious fist and shaking the final cashews and brazils vigorously. "Our company is so flat we hardly protrude above the horizon line. But it's also a way for people to get away with murder, especially if they're in a remote facility. You can talk about empowerment all you want, and I'm a believer in it. But I also know there are plenty of people who don't want to be empowered. They can't deal with the responsibility. They want you to tell them what to do, and then come back and check up on them and make sure they've done it."

I said nothing, and he fell silent for a moment, then started up again.

"I know that doesn't sound enlightened. But I believe that's the way it is. There are some fundamentals of big organizations that you simply can't change, no matter how much you talk about quality and empowerment and all the rest. Just read any business journal, and you'll find at least one article about how change efforts have failed."

"But some do succeed," I said. "They're the ones that matter."

"Maybe," said my seatmate, unconvinced. "Success is much more about who's in charge, and whether you're in the right business or not and whether you've got the right product, not whether you have a bunch of happy, empowered workers."

"How else do you get in the right business and create the right products, if your people don't help get you there?"

"Management sets strategy, and then you go ahead and implement. Your people don't have to be empowered and working in happy teams to implement effectively."

"How about to implement with imagination and innovation? And creativity."

"Are you an HR guy?" asked my seatmate, with a twinge of disdain.

"No," I said.

"Well," he said, and turned away to wave his empty nut bowl at the flight attendant, "you sure sound like it."

He was silent for another moment, then shifted his body toward me. "Teams are just another trendy management tool. It's just the next thing."

"Shouldn't we always be trying the next thing?"

"There's nothing new about it. It's just the same old fundamentals with new language wrapped around them."

"You don't believe in the fundamentals?"

"Of course I do."

"So what's the problem?"

My seatmate stared at me for a moment.

"The problem is that teamwork is nothing. Of course people work in teams. How else could they work? Teamwork makes for good business journal articles and fat consulting contracts and that's about it."

"Have you ever tried organizing your people into cross-functional teams?" I asked calmly.

"Of course we have. We've been through the whole quality thing. We had quality task forces and quality improvement teams and quality therapy sessions, and the whole thing, as far as I can tell, had virtually no effect. Except that now we have a flag flying out front of the home office with a Q on it."

He looked at me earnestly. "How about you?"

"You're looking at a team leader."

"I thought team leaders flew coach," he said, and snapped on the television.

FOXFILE ENTRY:

- The good opinion your team has of teamwork may not be shared or understood by others. If they won't listen, you can't make them understand. A good and different idea is logical only in hindsight. Only then will some people grasp it. But, by then, you should be on to the next good and different idea. Their ignorance is your competitive advantage.

52. *I Meet the Great Prandar.*

I arrived in Paris early, fumbled with my high school French (on some two hours of sleep), and secured a taxi. We roared through the Paris suburbs to the FCI office in St. Cloud, arriving there just past eight o'clock, FlyingFox clutched close to me as if it were a diplomatic valise.

Prandar was there when I arrived, a balding, middle-aged Pakistani man with a shy smile. Without saying good morning, he took the package and said, "Oh good." He led me to a little kitchen where I thankfully collected a large cup of coffee, a hard roll, and a croissant with jam.

Breakfast in hand, we repaired to a small, sunny workroom where we spent the next six hours together. I watched Prandar work. He did little but drink water, glance at his watch, tap at the keyboard, stare at the screen, sit back and rock in his chair, finger on lips, and occasionally download code into FlyingFox and then test its controls. I drank large quantities of coffee and struggled to keep awake. It was too early to make any calls back to the office.

Now and again, Prandar would giggle at the keyboard, or frown. Sometimes he would turn to me and make odd comments.

"Someone has made a dog's dinner of this," he said once.

Or, "There is no roundedness to this bit."

Or, "No matter what mathematicians say, I do not think mathematics is like music, do you?"

And sometimes he lapsed into his own language, that is to say, softwarese. He would ramble for minutes at a time in this language, which was far more difficult to penetrate than French.

At 2:16 (I remember checking the time on my watch, which actually still read 8:16) Prandar pushed away from the desk and rubbed his stomach. "I must be going," he said. "My plane leaves in forty minutes."

In my jet-lagged state, I tried to understand what his plans were. Did he think he could just leave without fixing our problem?

"How close are you to solving it?"

"I don't know," said Prandar. "That is impossible to know."

"Can you keep working on it?"

"I'll keep it with me on the flight to Canberra."

"Can't you postpone your trip?" I sounded desperate, even to myself.

"Impossible. I'm meeting with the minister of trade and industry."

"But what do you think the problem is?"

"If I knew I would have fixed it," said Prandar.

"But—"

"It is better that you know about the problem now rather than after it is on the market. This way you can simply kill the product," said Prandar, loading papers and disks into a leather handbag.

"We can't kill the product. We've been working on it for months. The whole TS Group is depending on it."

Prandar shrugged. He picked up his bag. "I hope that FCI does not rise or fall on any one product. That would be foolish." He patted FlyingFox. "Although I must say this is an interesting one."

"Yes, and a lot of customers are eager to get their hands on it."

"Oh," said Prandar, "we can't judge our efforts by the reaction of the customers. They are even less reliable than our own management."

He extended his hand. "I must be going. Will you ride with me to the airport?"

The flight home was one of the most miserable of my life. First class was unavailable. Business class was full. No amount of requests for upgrades, flashing of frequent flyer cards, ranting, or pleading could get me out of a middle seat positioned deep in coach. The movie screen was a scrap of paper at the greatest possible distance from my seat. The woman next to me had carried on three overstuffed string bags filled with duty-free goods. An unhappy child squirmed to my right. The man in front jolted his seat backward, nearly crushing my knees. A teenager behind kept kicking me.

I sat, rigid, and stared at the brilliant light playing across the plastic ceiling.

Prandar was right. FlyingFox was just one FCI product. It didn't matter that much. No, Prandar was wrong. FlyingFox mattered a great deal. It wasn't just a product, it was an important part of a whole new initiative. But maybe it didn't matter if FlyingFox got to market later. So what if we missed the management meeting and introduced it four or six weeks down the road? Yes, it did matter. If we missed the meeting, FlyingFox would not get the attention it deserved from the sales force. And, if we were later to market, MarTech might beat us there. Besides, the New World was supposed to mean Early to Market. Well, maybe it didn't matter if we dropped the voice response and went with pushbutton controls. The machine still had functional advantages over existing products. Yes, it did matter. Voice response was a critical element of Product Delight. Sure, but maybe it didn't matter if there were a few defective units in the marketplace. How many would fail, anyway? And would customers mind? Yes, it mattered. Quality mattered. But, in the long run, maybe it didn't matter if I got fired or had to retire early or if Team FlyingFox was publicly disgraced and humiliated. Yes, that mattered. What about Andrea and Nick and Phyllis? What about Kip and Emma and Janice? We had to find a solution. I had to find a solution.

It was past ten when we landed. I decided, on an impulse, to stop at the office on the way home. I exchanged tired words with the night guard and, as I was signing in, I heard a voice from somewhere in the back of the building. A woman's voice.

"Somebody here?" I asked.

"Yeah," said the guard, "some of those Fox people are in the back room."

As I made my way to the Lair, the woman's voice grew louder and more distinct. She was repeating, "Good morning," over and over again and then "I am ready," in a clear, distinct tone. "Ready!" Had I not spent twenty-four hours in a fruitless mission, and had I not been operating on two few hours of sleep, I would have realized immediately what the voice saying that simple word meant.

Wesley and Nick were sitting at the CAD terminal, surrounded by crushed soda cans and candy bar wrappers.

"Hi, Ron," Wes said nonchalantly when I came in. "How was the trip?" He kept his gaze on the two boxes before him: the CAD terminal and the FlyingFox prototype, its guts spewing onto the tabletop.

"Prandar's working on it," I said.

"He doesn't have to," said Nick, without looking at me.

"Why not?"

"We fixed it."

"What?"

"We fixed the problem."

"Who fixed the problem?"

Wesley turned to me, and now could see that I was not in full possession of my mental or physical powers.

"Ron, maybe you should sit down."

"I'm okay. If someone would just tell me what's going on." Nick turned to me as well, surprised by the nervous edge to my voice.

"Last night, after you left, we all got together. Nick, me, Andrea, the Sharks by video. Nelson."

"We just grabbed whoever we thought might be able to help," added Nick.

Wesley chuckled. "Even Zanoski was here."

"That was the first time I have ever seen him take off his tie," marveled Nick.

"Or eat potato chips."

I shook my head. "So Zanoski figured out the problem?"

"Nope," continued Wesley. "It was a group effort. But David Clair asked the critical question."

"Which led Wesley to hit upon the solution." Nick patted Wesley's brain.

"David Clair?" In my exhaustion, I couldn't place the name at first, then I remembered that he was my "first choice" engineer, the one who had turned me down. "How did *he* get involved in this?"

Nick laughed. "He was just passing by on his way home."

Wesley shook his head. "He said he smelled smoke in here. We said it was from a lot of overheated brains."

"But David told me he wasn't interested in FlyingFox technology," I said.

"I think he's changed his mind," said Nick.

They looked at me, as if waiting for praise. I could hardly react. "So what was the question he asked?"

"We had been assuming the problem was in the software or some hardware component that affected the software. But David simply asked, 'Could it be electrical?' And that's what it was. A short circuit caused by a tiny manufacturing fault. It was beautiful!"

I thought of my fruitless sojourn to Paris, the nervous hours with Prandar, my return-flight despair. "Beautiful? Engineers are a strange breed," I said.

Nick looked at me reproachfully. "Hey, Ron, that comes close to a UPA. Engineers may have caused the problem, but we also fixed it."

"Sorry," I said wearily, and stumbled over to the flipchart.

"What are you doing?" asked Wesley.

I picked up a marker. "Marking myself down for a UPA."

Wesley and Nick jumped up, and each took one of my tired elbows.

"Special dispensation this time, Ron," said Wesley.

"Can I drive you home?" said Nick.

"No, I think I'll just . . ."

Pass out on the couch.

"Good morning," said FlyingFox.

I awoke at noon the next day, to Janice gently nudging my elbow.

"Ron. Ron. Time to wake up."

I sat sharply upright.

"We'll fix it!" I blurted. "Don't worry!"

Janice rubbed my shoulder. "Jasper just called from Lyons."

"We're cancelled?"

"He called to congratulate you. He said the steering committee wants to make FlyingFox the focus of the management meeting."

"What?" Then I remembered that FlyingFox was still airborne.

"Jasper's just happy that I saved his ass," I said, flopping back into bed.

"He didn't mention his ass. He did say you had made a spectacular team effort," said Janice evenly.

"I wasn't even there."

"He said that's the mark of a great team. They carry on even when their leader is fallen, or stuck on an airplane. He told me that I ought to be proud of you."

"What did you say?" I asked, drifting back into sleep.

"I told him I already was."

53. *FlyingFox Is Launched.*

Eight days before the management meeting and FlyingFox launch, Kate ascended to a vice-presidency. Although she didn't officially leave the team, she might as well have, so absorbed was she in her new responsibilities. Andrea took over the management of all marketing communications activities, and did so superbly.

We introduced FlyingFox to the sales force in the morning session of the management meeting, and then, following a slightly different script, we made the FlyingFox presentation again, this time to the press, industry analysts, and a few key customers. Initial response was extremely positive. The sales force cheered. The press clapped politely. Four customers placed initial orders.

That evening, 627 Fickies gathered for dinner in the hotel ballroom, which had been converted into multimedia theater and banquet hall. The steering committee, including Jasper, Zanoski, Bill Ferry, and FCI founder Marshall Osgood, sat up front. And next to them, at what had been designated the table of honor, sat the FlyingFox team members, including Hartmut and Keith. We were flying high.

Ferry tapped his water glass with a butter knife.

"Could I have your attention, everyone. For a moment, please."

The chatter subsided. "Today," Ferry began, his voice nearly lost in the big room. "Can't hear ya, Bill!" somebody screamed from way in the back. A technician rushed to Ferry and handed him a wireless microphone. "Can you hear me now!?" Ferry boomed.

"Roger Wilco!" called the voice to pilot Ferry.

"Today," Ferry continued, giving a general thumbs-up to the crowd, "we have begun to see the payoff on our investment in teamwork. It gave me a tremendous feeling of pride to see the first of the New World products go to market, and go to market early. Let's hear it for FlyingFox."

Warm applause, but not overwhelming. The room was filled with members of other New World teams, after all.

"FlyingFox is the first manifestation of the three objectives we set ourselves many months ago. It has Product Delight. In a big way."

The Foxes laughed.

"It is Early to Market. Not even that pesky little company—what are they called?" said Ferry, pretending to forget MarTech's name. He looked at us, and we all shrugged.

"BarCheck, or whatever that company's name is—they don't have anything remotely like FlyingFox."

Cheers for FlyingFox mixed with boos for MarTech.

"And, finally and equally important, FlyingFox was developed by a cross-functional team, one that was chartered only a few months ago. And it's one hell of a team. Team FlyingFox!"

More-than-polite applause. Ferry applauded, too, his claps amplified dramatically by the mike in his hand. We waved.

"Not only did they figure out how to work together, they overcame a series of technical and process challenges along the way. I know, because I watched them do it." Ferry paused and looked at us with genuine pride. "So, FlyingFox is the first. And I'd say it's a pretty decent model for the other New World teams to follow. So, to all of you," he said, looking at us, "our congratulations, thanks, and admiration."

Now Jasper stood and reached for the mike. "Just keep it under forty-five minutes, will you, Jasper?" said Ferry.

Ripples of knowing laughter. "Thank you, Bill," said Jasper, his eyes twinkling. "Let me add that what we are celebrating tonight is not just FlyingFox. What is happening at FCI these days, right before our astonished eyes, is that dreaded phenomenon we call change. What is wonderful about it, however, is that it's change for the better, and it's change brought about in good measure by the New World teams. People ask me if the New World teams are going to last. Quite often, I must confess, the question comes from the team members themselves."

Laughter from us.

"And I say to them, yes they're going to last, as long as they can work as effectively as Team FlyingFox, and as long as they can get results. Look at Ron and Phyllis and Wesley and Nick and Andrea and Nelson and their colleagues from Shark Design and you are looking at the future of FCI. I know it's frightening, but it's true! So, one more round of applause for the Foxes, and then I want to see some healthy and murderous competition from the rest of you!"

More applause. And then our moment in the spotlight was over. The chatter resumed.

Andrea raised her glass to me. "Let's hear it for the Tallest Team Leader!" They cheered. Glasses were raised to lips. But no one drank. Glasses hovered and eyes were fixed at a point just over my left shoulder. I felt a heavy hand there. I turned. It was Dr. Osgood.

"Hello, Foxes," he said. Osgood is a blunt-figured man of middle height. His white hair is usually in as much disarray as his cotton suits. He clutched a tumbler of clear liquid, his signature martini.

"Does anybody at this table know what the letters FCI stand for?" asked Osgood.

It was Phyllis who mustered her courage first. "Fungible Company Incorporated."

"What's your name?" asked Osgood.

"Phyllis," she said, "from purchasing."

"Phyllis, you're right," said Osgood. "Fungible Company Inc. And do you know why we picked that name?"

"Not really," said Phyllis.

"Because a fungible thing is such that one part can be replaced by another part, in order to get the job done," said Osgood. "If the parts of your organization are fungible, then the whole organization is flexible. Do you see what I'm getting at?"

Not exactly. But it was so rare that Osgood, founder of one of the greatest American companies, talked about anything for any length of time that we were prepared to listen to him no matter what he said.

"FCI wasn't like a lot of companies that were founded to

do just one thing. I didn't want to just make microchips or railroad spikes or ice cream cones. When we were founded, I envisioned a company that could be flexible, one that could change over time. A company where you would be able to make a contribution greater than you imagined you ever could. And, if you didn't," he added, "you were gone." He chuckled. "My, it was a lot easier to fire people in those days."

He paused and shook his head. "Anyway, I think that's pretty much the way we were for the first couple of decades. We managed to have a little fun and make some money, too."

He took a sip of his martini, and paused. "Then we got big. We got successful. And the board did what boards like to do. They made a big mistake and forced me into retirement. FCI became fat and sluggish. But I didn't!"

We laughed politely, thinking about the bloodbath that had surrounded the forced-retirement episode. Osgood changed conversational course.

"I find it amusing that everybody's talking about teams these days. The hot management topic." He scoffed. "We were a team forty years ago. In a garage!"

He swirled the gin around in his glass and gazed at the rug, then looked up at all of us with an unexpectedly piercing glance.

"The trick, you know, is to keep it going. That's the hard part. So, take my advice, and keep yourselves fungible!"

He smiled broadly. "Now let's see if you can't sell a few million of these Foxes of yours. The share price is eight points lower than it should be. And I still own twenty-six million shares, you know."

Founder and legend Osgood marched off and was soon engulfed by dozens of Fickies wanting to have a word with him.

The Foxes looked at each other uncertainly. Had we been praised or had we been chastised? We didn't care. Team FlyingFox was a success. We had entered into the lore and mythology of the great and venerable FCI tribe.

Hail to the Foxes

It was April again, just about a year after we had launched the FlyingFox product, and nearly two years after we had first formed the FlyingFox team. One rare day when the pace slackened and I had an hour to spare, I found myself in the Lair browsing through the FoxFile. Reading some of my notes, reviewing the minutes of the tenser meetings, and glancing through the E-mail messages that had been saved. The first two were the most recent:

To: Ron
From: Jasper

Just reviewed the sales results for the year. How is it possible that FlyingFox achieved 142% of forecast in its first year of life? And how is it possible that the order book is strong for the next three quarters, and that, even with this unexpected demand, you're averaging delivery within seven days of order? And that your profit margins are essentially on target?

How is it possible to have any doubts that your team is a success?

To: Shark Design
From: Team FlyingFox

We are delighted to hear that FlyingFox has been selected as a product of the year by *Business Week* and the Industrial Designers Society of America. It's almost embarrassing after already receiving the same honor from IOSTF. We have noticed that Product Delight has become an industry-standard term, and that FlyingFox is the embodiment of it.

What do we do for an encore?

Our success was especially satisfying when considered in the light of our uncertain beginnings. I remembered the early questions. Why did we need teams? Who would lead them? What effect would membership have on our careers? Could we achieve results? Now, two years later, many of the questions had been answered.

FlyingFox was a highly successful and visible product and had helped FCI dramatically improve its position in the office systems market. In a direct way, therefore, the team strategy had helped achieve a key corporate objective.

Team FlyingFox was still going strong, although its mission had changed. Now, rather than developing new products, we were primarily focused on product management—manufacturing, marketing, and servicing FlyingFox.

Accordingly, the composition of the team had changed as well. We had recruited a new person with expertise in distribution and selling channels. We also were planning a line extension and some ancillary products. But our designer, Nick Yu, had left FCI and taken a job at Shark Design, so David Clair volunteered to take his place. As Jasper put it, FlyingFox had made converts of even the most cynical antiteam Fickies.

With his healthy commissions from FlyingFox, Cub bought a classic Ford Falcon, in tribute to the power of the doubleF.

Wes looker trimmer and more enthusiastic than I had seen him in years, and now enjoyed a reputation as *the* Fickie engineer.

Dick Eggart stayed with FCI after Ficus was cancelled, but he was soon transferred out of corporate and into the accounting department of a struggling subsidiary. When he heard rumors that the subsidiary might be sold, Dick cashed in his stock, took early retirement, and opened a fishing tackle shop in Egypt, Maine.

Her work with FlyingFox computer systems catapulted Phyllis into a new career. She left purchasing and joined the MIS organization, working as assistant to Jocelyn Veens. Nights, Phyllis studied at the local business college toward a degree in computer science. Barry said it was okay by him.

Dr. Zanoski was honored for his development of FungiFlex and had just been nominated for the Inventors Hall of Fame. The image of R&D changed radically, and FCI was becoming known as an innovative company once again. We like to kid Dr. Z about the night he ate potato chips and loosened his tie.

Martha continued her steady rise. She left C&P to take Ferry's old job as head of European operations, and was considered the favorite to move into the president's slot if and when Ferry moved up to chairman.

Carlos, we heard, had moved to a new job, this one in

Italy. Someone who had spoken with him said he was doing well but was still a little peevish.

Andrea's able handling of the FlyingFox launch had earned her widespread recognition. At Jasper's urging, she had taken a new position in the Midwest office, heading up a team there. Not only did this bring her greater responsibility and better compensation, it brought her closer to Keith.

Kate was not around to make good on my bet with her. Once she became a vice-president, she set her sights on Jasper's job as group chief. After a fierce struggle, however, Jasper prevailed and Kate left the company in a huff. Within a couple of months she surfaced—as executive vice-president at FCI's archrival, MarTech.

Then J. Sanford Picker, MarTech's CEO, got mixed up in a stock manipulation scandal and left the company in disgrace. Kate found herself jockeying for the top job, after only two months at her new company.

Not long ago, we got an E-mail from Prandar. The message read, "Your problem is not in the software." It's always nice to have a genius available.

And me? Two years earlier, Martha had told me that I would have to change to be a successful team leader. Perhaps the best evidence that I had changed was to be found in a piece of news coverage we had received.

FlyingFox, product and team, had been featured in *The Wall Street Journal* about two months earlier. The front-page headline read OLD FOX FINDS NEW MARKET. The subheadline added, "Invigorated FCI Gets Results From Cross-Functional Product Development Teams." And the sub-sub-headline: "Welcome to the New World."

The story traced the development of FlyingFox and its success in the marketplace. William J. Ferry, Jasper S. Lash, and Ronald M. Delaney were quoted saying nice things about each other, the importance of teamwork, and the product itself. About halfway down the column was a photograph (actually a *Journal*-style lithograph based on a photograph) of Team FlyingFox. There we were, arms slung around each other, the product proudly placed in the foreground, Emma's fierce FlyingFox logo prominent on our team T-shirts.

Just two years ago I had pictured myself on the cover of

Fortune, a Courageous Captain and Lone Warrior, similar to J. Sanford Picker. But in the *Wall Street Journal* photo I stood modestly in the background, the Tall Team Leader, smiling a proud, avuncular smile. It wasn't a *Fortune* cover, but it was better than the imaginary headline that had jolted me into volunteering: NICE SMART GUY PLODS ALONG.

One last thing. As hard as we tried, we never could determine how the rumors about FlyingFox were leaked, or by whom.

Nobody said teams can solve everything.

Ron's Reading List of Team Books

These are a few of the books I read during the two years I was leader of Team FlyingFox:

Competitive Advantage, by Michael E. Porter. Smart discussion of how corporations compete in their markets.

The Corporation of the 1990s, edited by Michael S. Scott Morton. How corporate structures are changing and the role of technology.

The Fifth Discipline, by Peter Senge. The corporation as a "learning organization."

Future Perfect, by Stanley E. Davis. Brainy stuff about how we're going to be (or should be) operating in the future.

In the Age of the Smart Machine, by Shosana Zuboff. Zuboff coined the word *informating* that Carlos talked about.

Leading Business Teams, by Robert Johansen and other contributors. The subtitle says it: "How teams can use technology and group process tools to enhance performance."

Managing for the Future, by Peter F. Drucker. Drucker is a wise man.

Mining Group Gold, by Thomas A. Kayser. Nuts and bolts of teamwork.

My Years with General Motors, by Alfred P. Sloan, Jr. Sloan presided over the development of the hierarchical organization and speaks lucidly about its benefits and problems.

Ragged Dick, by Horatio Alger. Getting ahead is simple: Work hard, be smart, be honest, save your money, get up early. One of the first business novels.

Rethinking the Corporation: The Architecture of Change, by Robert M. Tomasko. A "big think" book on how to achieve a new "architecture" for the corporation.

Self-Directed Work Teams, by Jack Orsburn and other contributors. Thoughtful all-purpose discussion of all phases of teams.

Serious Creativity, by Edward de Bono. How to think, be creative, and solve problems alone and in groups.

Survival of the Fittest, by Philip A. Himmelfarb. Has a clear, concise chapter on how teams can contribute to business survival.

The Team Handbook, by Peter R. Scholtes and other contributors. A fat, well-designed, user-friendly workbook and handbook.

The Wheels of Commerce, by Fernand Braudel. If you really want to get the long view, Braudel takes you back to the very beginning of trade and commerce.

Workplace Teams, Leaders Guide for the AMA Partnership Video Series. Clear, straightforward, and helpful.